PRAISE FOR *BEYOND AWKWARD SIDE HUGS*

"The church desperately needs a bigger vision for how men and women can flourish together in ministry and friendship, and Bronwyn Lea paints a vivid picture for how we'll get there. Filled with grace, wisdom, and humor, *Beyond Awkward Side Hugs* is a trumpet blast for change and renewal."

—**Steve Wiens**, author of *Shining Like the Sun, Beginnings,* and *Whole*

"*Beyond Awkward Side Hugs* is a deep well of biblical wisdom, and Lea has written with nuance and clarity, humor and grace. Rather than spoon-feed rules, Lea offers a more patient and pastoral approach, helping readers form the skills of discernment. Her practical examples, mined from a life of ministry, are coupled with insightful questions sure to spark animated conversations about sex and dating, marriage and ministry, friendship and singleness. I look forward to being a student of Lea's teaching and writing in the years to come."

—**Jen Pollock Michel**, author of *Surprised by Paradox* and *Keeping Place*

"Ever since Adam first uttered the accusation 'It was that woman you gave me,' the relationship between men and women has been fraught with fractures. For millennia, humanity has swung between legalism and libertinism, and this overcorrection continues in the church today. Thankfully, Bronwyn Lea is offering a far better way. In these pages, Lea navigates the stormy waters of gender and sexuality with wisdom, scriptural insight, balance, conviction, and good humor. This book is a tremendous resource to anyone wanting to imitate the radical way of Jesus, but I especially commend it to leaders in the church. It is a much-needed word for our time."

—**Sharon Hodde Miller**, author of *Nice: Why We Love to Be Liked and How God Calls Us to More*

"Goodness, Bronwyn is a courageous writer; guiding us into a conversation where, these days, even angels fear to tread. With hard-won wisdom and deep compassion, these pages invite us to embrace each other's presence and gifts without shame or fear. We need one another, and we need writers like Bronwyn Lea."

—**Winn Collier**, author of *Love Big, Be Well*

"Given the central importance of the church's relational life for its own health and witness, it's amazing how little, genuinely useful, practical theology is written in this area. Ironically, conversations about faithful human sexuality all too easily become abstract and unrelational. And so, I'm thankful for Bronwyn Lea's book, which comes as a breath of fresh air and will be a great resource for the church and its people. Writing as a 'relational theologian,' Lea embraces our challenge of living as both sexual beings and brothers and sisters in Christ. Her insightful perspective, sharp humor, and practical stories help us to see this radical vision of church, not just as a biblical imperative, but as an incarnate and embodied reality."

—**Rev. Jonathan Grant**, author of *Divine Sex*

"This was an exciting and necessary read for me, given the current state of relationships between men and women. How does anyone navigate relationships with the opposite sex without retreating in chilly distance or the creepy opposite? With piercing insight and streetwise wisdom, Bronwyn has charted a course forward that gives me great hope for the church to lead the way in relational warmth and mutuality between men and women. The truly great gift, however, is how these are not mere ivory tower pontifications because I have personally witnessed and experienced how Bronwyn herself has lived this out in her home church."

—**Steve Luxa**, senior pastor of First Baptist Church of Davis

"Words that come to mind having just finished reading, Beyond Awkward Side Hugs: refreshing, honest, healthy, robust, and needed. Bronwyn Lea writes with relatable examples, timely humor, and insightful biblical scholarship. Having also worked and ministered with youth, college, young adults, newly married, singles, and now empty-nesters, I am grateful for this book during a time when so much confusion surrounds the relationships shared between women and men. Bronwyn offers perspective, wisdom, and a call for us move past awkward to the example lived out by Jesus himself. We are created for relationship and community and the richness found in meaningful connection is available between men and women in the family of God."

—**Vivian Mabuni**, speaker, podcast host, and author of *Open Hands, Willing Heart*

BEYOND

[AWKWARD]

SIDE HUGS

BEYOND

[AWKWARD]

SIDE HUGS

LIVING AS CHRISTIAN BROTHERS
AND SISTERS IN A SEX-CRAZED WORLD

BRONWYN LEA

NELSON
BOOKS

An Imprint of Thomas Nelson

Published in Nashville, Tennessee, by Nelson Books, an imprint of Thomas Nelson. Nelson Books and Thomas Nelson are registered trademarks of HarperCollins Christian Publishing, Inc.

Thomas Nelson titles may be purchased in bulk for educational, business, fund-raising, or sales promotional use. For information, please e-mail SpecialMarkets@ThomasNelson.com.

Unless otherwise noted, Scripture quotations are taken from the ESV® Bible (The Holy Bible, English Standard Version®). Copyright © 2001 by Crossway, a publishing ministry of Good News Publishers. Used by permission. All rights reserved.

Scripture quotations marked THE MESSAGE are from *The Message*. Copyright © by Eugene H. Peterson 1993, 1994, 1995, 1996, 2000, 2001, 2002. Used by permission of NavPress. All rights reserved. Represented by Tyndale House Publishers, Inc.

Scripture quotations marked NIV are from the Holy Bible, New International Version®, NIV®. Copyright © 1973, 1978, 1984, 2011 by Biblica, Inc.® Used by permission of Zondervan. All rights reserved worldwide. www.Zondervan.com. The "NIV" and "New International Version" are trademarks registered in the United States Patent and Trademark Office by Biblica, Inc.®

Scripture quotations marked CSB are taken from the Christian Standard Bible®, Copyright © 2017 by Holman Bible Publishers. Used by permission. Christian Standard Bible® and CSB® are federally registered trademarks of Holman Bible Publishers.

Scripture quotations marked NLT are from the Holy Bible, New Living Translation. © 1996, 2004, 2007, 2013, 2015 by Tyndale House Foundation. Used by permission of Tyndale House Publishers, Inc., Carol Stream, Illinois 60188. All rights reserved.

Any Internet addresses, phone numbers, or company or product information printed in this book are offered as a resource and are not intended in any way to be or to imply an endorsement by Thomas Nelson, nor does Thomas Nelson vouch for the existence, content, or services of these sites, phone numbers, companies, or products beyond the life of this book.

ISBN 978-1-4002-1501-0 (eBook)
ISBN 978-1-4002-1500-3 (TP)

Library of Congress Control Number: 2019953579

Printed in the United States of America
20 21 22 23 24 LSC 10 9 8 7 6 5 4 3 2 1

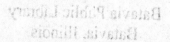

For my brothers and sisters at FBC.

CONTENTS

CONTENT

FOREWORD

BY CHRISTINE CAINE

I was the first woman ever to be appointed as the state director of our denomination's youth movement. It was the mid-1990s and I was in my late twenties at the time. I felt so honored and excited. I was full of vision, passion, and determination. I wanted nothing more than to reach unchurched Australian students with the gospel. I looked forward to working with our national youth executive team to see this dream come to pass.

When I went to the first national meeting of all the state directors, I was ready to contribute, to listen, to pray, and to plan our strategy together, but as I had always found at most every leadership gathering, I was the only woman at the table. And this time, it was a table full of married men, and I was a single woman. These were godly men, committed to the young people in their home states, but they had never sat at a decision-making table where a woman was present. And I do mean *never*.

Before any of our sessions began, the man seated on my right literally moved his chair several inches farther away from me, so we would not be sitting too close to one another. He didn't seem to mind that this meant he was virtually sitting on the lap of the state director seated on his other side. Another man did not even make eye contact with me—not once. Still another awkwardly shook my hand, but only for a brief second, and one man barely spoke during the meeting because, as I later found out, he felt weird that there was a woman even in the room. A woman who was not a secretary, but a peer in every way. He said to one of our colleagues, "I don't know how to talk to a woman who is not my wife. I don't want to be tempted and fall into sin."

When someone later told me what he said, I was absolutely flabbergasted. I had not even considered such a possibility. I was at the table to talk about youth ministry, about all of the plans and dreams we each had for reaching the lost and the unchurched in our states. I was not there to find a husband, especially if he was already someone else's husband. I am not sure what that man thought would happen if we had a conversation, but I can assure you I wouldn't have been tempted in any way and fallen into sin.

These men were the leaders of the next generation, and this was my first encounter with the challenges of living and working faithfully as Christian brothers and sisters in Christ. If we, as leaders in the church, could not get it right working together, what hope did the next generation have?

For the next seven years I served as a state director, and, in all those years, none of these men ever got in a car with me, unless there were several of them together. I was never invited to any post meeting social gatherings—all because I was a woman and single. To be faithful to the call of God meant that I was excluded from interactions that were vital to the work we were doing. I feel sure none of them ever considered the isolation or pain I felt at being excluded, and no one ever talked about the underlying assumptions that allowed this dysfunctional behavior to thrive.

At that time there was very little I could do about it, but despite all the awkwardness and exclusion, I chose to stay in the system so I could hopefully change some things for the young women coming after me. For the young women who were also called by God and who wanted to be in ministry.

So, for seven years I worked hard to break down these crazy invisible walls and create a healthy space where we could thrive together as men and women fulfilling the call of God. It was not easy, nor was I totally successful, but I remember thinking back then that someone needed to write a book about this dynamic because Christians are weird when it comes to men and women relating to one another. We need to do better for the sake of the Church. We should do better for the sake of our witness.

It's been more than twenty years since then, and I don't think we have made near the progress we should in this area, but I do think that *Beyond Awkward Side Hugs* is the book I have been waiting for to help us make headway.

Bronwyn masterfully shows us that "living faithfully as men and women—as inherently sexual beings—is every Christian disciple's responsibility." This book contributes to this vital conversation in such a powerful way. Bronwyn weaves together beautiful storytelling, hard data, and personal experience to show us a way forward. This is one of the most pressing issues of our time and we cannot ignore it any longer. My hope is that this book will help us all to "move beyond awkwardness and become familiar with each other—well acquainted and comfortable in our interactions—as family ought to be."

Your Sister in Christ,
Christine Caine

INTRODUCTION

LOST IN AWKWARDVILLE

Sunday mornings can be the best of times and the worst of times for Christian men and women. One particularly memorable morning highlighted both extremes. After church I spotted a friend I hadn't seen in years—a college buddy I'd known long before I was married. I swooped across the courtyard and was met with one of the giant, warm hugs I remembered so well. Two seconds later—still mid-hug—I began to feel painfully self-conscious. Thoughts raced through my head:

> *How long is this hug going to last? What will people think?*
> *What example is this setting for the students I've just been*
> *   chatting with, who see me as a leader?*
> *Will people assume he's an ex-boyfriend?*
> *What am I communicating with a hug?*
> *Does it still mean the same thing now as it did ten years ago?*

Should I have given him a side hug instead, since I'm married? Does he even know I'm married? Speaking of married, where is my husband?

And who is the insecure-looking woman standing to the side? Is she his girlfriend?

I backed out of the hug awkwardly. I didn't want people to *assume* things.

"So, was that your brother?" a student asked later, her question confirming I hadn't worried for nothing. I paused before answering. "Um . . . kind of." Because, in truth, he is. He's been a spiritual brother to me for over twenty years. But we live in a world where things can be clumsy and confusing between Christian men and women, and we can quickly feel lost in Awkwardville when it comes to how we relate to one another.

In the thirty-plus years I've been in church circles, I've heard all sorts of advice about how to relate to members of the opposite sex. For the most part, this advice has consisted of the "don't have sex until you're married" warnings for singles, and "only have sex with your spouse" for marrieds. It's like wanting to get from San Diego to New York City and only getting "make sure you don't fall into the Grand Canyon," and "turn left when you reach the Atlantic" as pointers. However true such advice might be, it's also frustratingly incomplete. The question "When and with whom can I have sex?" is a fundamentally different one from, "How can Christian men and women be in healthy relationships?"

As someone who's spent years in pastoral ministry, I've fielded my fair share of tricky sex-related questions. Figuring out what the Bible says about the right context for sex is relatively easy. Answer: in marriage. Figuring out how to handle our sexuality in a broader range of relationships is less straight-forward. However, whether I'm talking with the college-aged adults who pull up a stool at our kitchen counter, sitting down with someone at church who needs a pastoral ear, or answering questions from readers on email, the themes are surprisingly similar. A lot of us are confused, lonely, in pain, or frustrated. And even if we're clear on what the Bible says about the when and with whom of sex, we have *a lot* of follow-up questions.

We want to navigate relationships faithfully as Christians, but we're not sure how our sexuality fits into that. Or how our faith equips us to interact in meaningful ways with the men and women around us. We want to know whether we can hug an old friend after church without raising anyone's adultery alarms, for example. We have everyday questions, and we need guidance. We need help moving beyond awkward side hugs, through the rugged terrain of our sex-crazed culture, and into the open plains of living as Christian brothers and sisters.

WHICH WAY IS NORTH?

The sexual landscape is changing so quickly these days, which only confuses things further. We might not feel that old, but when we hear about twelve-year-olds sending nude pictures to each other on smartphones, we realize just how much and how rapidly the world has changed. Everything seems to be so much more sexually charged than it was before, and technology seems to be accelerating these changes at alarming rates. We have mixed feelings about the internet and social media. We're grateful for the relational connection they offer, but leery of the internet's underbelly and how it reflects—and, what's more, refuels—the sex-focused world we live in. The relational and sexual terrain has shifted, and it's hard to find our bearings.

With more and more stories of sex-gone-wrong in the spotlight, we rightly worry about the health of our own relationships. We read about #MeToo and #ChurchToo as we scroll through our news feeds, where yet another pastor or priest has been accused of sexual misconduct or abuse. "Not again," we sigh, and we wonder if the church will someday speak with credibility on the topic of men, women, and sexuality. We second-guess interactions we ourselves have had in the past.

To make matters worse, we are flooded with a dizzying number of conflicting messages. On Saturday nights we might tune in to watch our favorite shows on Netflix or HBO—perhaps *Game of Thrones* or *Grey's Anatomy*—with all their sex and steamy relationships in vivid color. We know these shows are entertainment and that the characters are not appropriate role models for us as Christians, but we feel our desires stoked by such stories and wonder what to do with those longings.

Just hours later on Sunday morning, we sit in a church where no one has said or taught anything about sex or sexuality for years, except maybe to hint that men need accountability groups for porn. We see a gaping disconnect between church on Sunday and our lived experience Monday to Saturday and, like a driver getting conflicting directions from the map app on their phone and the outdated map in the glove compartment, we wonder which way to go.

Perhaps, since we don't hear much at church about living faithfully in our sexuality as men and women, we look to other Christians for wisdom. We read about the "Billy Graham

Rule," which stipulates never spending time alone with a member of the opposite sex except one's spouse. But we wonder how workable such a practice is in our everyday lives. We have male and female coworkers, and fellow parents at school we want to connect with. Do we really have to avoid being alone with Rachel in the lunch room, or talking to John while our kids are playing baseball? Can we go to a mixed-sex Bible study, or will that be a "distraction"? And how do we respond to a single friend in her thirties or forties who says she just can't come to church anymore because it feels like the marrieds are closing ranks, and she feels lonelier on Sunday mornings than any other time of the week?

LONELY IN A CROWD

We have so many questions and so many hurts. It breaks my heart to hear people say they've left church because they didn't feel there was space for someone in their situation. Too often that situation is related to relationships and sexuality—they're not sure there's a place for them if they aren't part of a husband-wife pair in a traditional nuclear family. I'm devastated hearing Christians—both married and unmarried—tell me again and again that they feel fundamentally *lonely* at church, even though they're surrounded by people on Sunday mornings. Why is this such a common experience?

Often, it's the fear of "getting it wrong"—of being misunderstood or creating confusion—that keeps us from reaching out to make friends with the men and women around us, even though we deeply long for close relationships. We don't want to be the weird, uptight Christians who never say yes to party invitations, but we also don't want our marriages and churches rent apart at the seams—and isn't that how things always seem to go when men and women become friends?

Why *can't* we just be friends? It seems like it shouldn't be that hard. But then we remember our divorced friend recovering from heartbreak, or the pain we ourselves carry from a sexual betrayal at the hands of parents, a spouse, or leaders. *Maybe it's safer to not even try*, we think. And so we retreat into the one little space where we know it's okay to seek relationship: with our spouse, if we have one. But one relationship—no matter how great it is—doesn't feel like enough. We feel stuck. We're not sure if there is a safe space for our longings or our lingering questions in our Christian communities. So we withdraw. We see an old friend, and we're too afraid to give them a hug.

THE TOPIC THAT JUST WON'T GO AWAY

If you'd told me twenty years ago that I'd write a book on relationships—and *sexuality* in relationships, at that—I would have thrown back my head and laughed. I was already much more Calvin's *Institutes* than *Teen Vogue* in my reading habits, drawn to conversations about truth and justice over questionnaires rating celebrities on a hotness scale. I'd already turned my back on a legal career and responded to God's call to disciple and teach the Bible to women in my church. I was a seminary student, passionate about equipping people to understand and apply the Scriptures. I was neck-deep in classes ending in "-etics"—homiletics, exegetics, hermeneutics, and more. I was gearing up for my calling as Gospel Girl, whether or not that role came with a superhero cape.

But twenty years of conversations with Christians have convinced me that the issue of sexuality in relationships is not a fringe topic or a topic to be set aside in favor of more "spiritual" issues. In fact, I have come to believe it is an unavoidably central part of how we live out the gospel. Questions about how we build relationships at the intimate level of sex in marriage, as well as at the broadest levels of church ministry and evangelism, *all* require a theological foundation for what it means to be a man or a woman—created with sexuality—and how to live that out in community.

> SEXUALITY IN RELATIONSHIPS IS NOT A FRINGE TOPIC OR A TOPIC TO BE SET ASIDE IN FAVOR OF MORE "SPIRITUAL" ISSUES.

What we believe about who we are and how we relate to each other as men and women *matters*. It matters missionally for the global mobilization of the church, and it matters pastorally for our spiritual formation. I have yet to be in a mentoring relationship that *hasn't* included conversation about what God says about this or that aspect of one's own sexuality and how it affects relationships. Any gospel ministry worth its salt has to grapple with the questions devoted Christians have about navigating their sexuality in a sex-drenched world. We all know of "private" sexual behavior that has caused nuclear-bomb-level public devastation. Years of Christian ministry can be undone by one affair. Faithfulness with our sexuality is very much a gospel issue.

The church has many resources for Christian men and women expressing their sexuality as wives and husbands. But long before we are wives and husbands (if that is something God has for us), we need to learn to handle ourselves as men and women around each other. Living faithfully as men and women—as inherently sexual beings—is every Christian disciple's responsibility. And the conversation about stewarding our sexuality isn't done and dusted if we happen to get married—husbands and wives still need a framework for living as men and women in a world that is unavoidably populated by other men and women. There's just no escaping sexuality—our own, or that of others.

On our wedding day, my husband promised himself to me alone, "forsaking all others," in the language of our vows. However, that forsaking applies only to his taking of other wives and sexual partners. It does not mean forsaking relationships with any and all women. Half the world's population is women, and as a disciple of Christ, he is called to love, serve, help, encourage, and partner with other Christians—not just the "unforsaken" half of the population in the men's ministry. And even though I promised myself to him alone—forsaking all other spouses and sexual partners—I still need to figure out how to love, serve, help, encourage, and partner with both men and women for Jesus' sake.

Can it be tricky? Yes. Will people sometimes misunderstand? Yes. Is it risky? Yes, there is always risk where imperfect humans are involved. Is there the possibility of sexual tension and sin? Yes. Is it sometimes awkward? Yes. Do we need to try anyway? Absolutely, yes. Because even though we may not have known it at the beginning of our story, God has given us a fundamental truth that puts all our relationships into a new light: *we are brothers and sisters in God's family*. That means we find a way to be close without being sexual. We can move beyond awkwardness and become familiar with each other—well-acquainted and comfortable in our interactions—as family ought to be.

The world we live in is conditioned to see the erotic possibilities in any human interaction, but it doesn't have to be that way for us. As men and women who are followers of Christ, our options aren't limited to the extremes of "zero contact" or "full frontal." In God's household, we have a third way: the way of family.

PART I

GETTING OUR BEARINGS

CHAPTER 1

AWKWARD, LONELY, AND OVERSEXED

CHRISTIANS AND CULTURE AS UNLIKELY BEDFELLOWS

Adam and Bronwyn, sitting in a tree, k-i-s-s-i-n-g,
    First comes love, then comes marriage,
    Then comes baby in a baby carriage."

It starts early and it's everywhere: the idea that any boy and any girl showing each other attention will lead to all that k-i-s-s-i-n-g stuff. I was one of a throng of six-year-olds singing this song to my friends, even though I blushed when it was sung of me. Adam and I were skipping, hand in hand, as six-year-olds sometimes do. No big deal. But the schoolyard ditty suggested it was maybe a bigger deal than we realized. No matter how much we protested that we were *just skipping*, the teasing continued. The awkwardness grew, until one day it didn't seem worth it to skip together anymore. Which was a pity. I liked skipping. I think he did too.

The lessons we learn at age six stay with us. Even as adults we are on high alert when a man and a woman show each other attention. Will it lead to all that k-i-s-s-i-n-g stuff? If we are at the age and stage of dating, perhaps we hope the answer is yes. But for the vast majority of our other interactions, we're cautious about those relationships. Few of us have escaped the pain of male-female relationships gone wrong—marriages rent by infidelity and churches split over sexual misconduct, pornography addiction damaging families and abusive power dynamics in the workplace, just to mention a few. The explosive power of sex is felt everywhere, and we are conflicted—we are drawn to the fireworks but rightly fear dynamite detonating in our hands.

LIVING IN A SEX-CRAZED WORLD

Somewhere between coaxing us through the horrors of *Macbeth* and coaching us in the mind-numbing work of diagramming sentences, my high school English teacher taught a unit on visual literacy. She distributed copies of a glossy magazine page and directed our attention not to the words but to the picture: a muscled sprinter crouched in a starting position on a racetrack—wearing patent red stiletto heels. The picture was an ad for premium car tires. "Power is nothing without control," the caption read.

"What is this picture telling you?" my teacher asked. "And what is it selling you?"

In this case, the message was clear: a powerful car without great tires is as pointless as a sprinter in stilettos. Nodding her encouragement, my teacher passed out ad after ad, prodding us to look deeper and write down our observations. "What about this one?" she asked. "What does it appeal to? What does it make you want? How does the product suggest it can meet that desire?" Slowly, we learned the habits of reading both *text* and the much less obvious, but far more persuasive, *subtext*.

Until I did this exercise, I didn't realize how much sex appeal really *appealed* most everywhere and to everyone. Appalled, I found myself writing some version of the same answer over and over again: *This advertiser is appealing to our need to belong and be found attractive. The subtext communicates that if you buy this deodorant, car, perfume, phone, or pair of jeans, you will be irresistible to the opposite sex and thus be happy and fulfilled.* Once I was aware of how advertisers used sex to sell their products, I noticed it everywhere. Our teacher supplied the word I was reaching for: *ubiquitous*. It's an adjective that means existing everywhere at the same time. In other words, we can't escape it—sex is ubiquitous.

Our society is hypersexualized, excessively concerned with the sexual possibility (or threat) in every interaction. Deodorant isn't just deodorant; it's the scent that will make you irresistible. Cars aren't just cars; they're vehicles for making road-trip memories with the hot partner of your dreams. Music lyrics move from dance floor to tangled sheets in two rhymed verses. Dozens of TV sitcoms teach us how romance goes: a guy and girl who are friends—roommates, coworkers, neighbors—suffer through missed connections, double entendres, and unrequited feelings, inevitably leading to a season finale that culminates with *the kiss* (or sex) to relieve the tension. Sexual chemistry is the subtext for many of the images we see and the stories we absorb.

It was Sigmund Freud, the father of psychoanalysis, who laid the groundwork for our sex-focused culture. Freud considered sexual desire, which he called *libido*, and repressed sexual desire as driving forces in virtually every human interaction from infancy to old age. Freud's legacy has lingered long, and we have become a society trained to suspect sexual undertones most everywhere. He would, I think, feel quite vindicated at how we see sex in the subtext of glossy magazine ads. And perhaps he would commend the fact that even close friendships of old are now read through a deconstructionist lens: surely Jonathan and David weren't *just friends*, right? Thanks to Freud, the nudge-nudge, wink-wink moments in our conversations almost always bend toward innuendo.

In second grade, I wrote a poem about a circus clown that included the line, "Here he comes / happy and gay / just listen to what he has to say." There may or may not have been appallingly bad accompanying artwork. Sister Marta, a nun and my favorite teacher, liked my poem enough to submit it for publication in the annual school magazine. I hardly imagine my rhymed verse would be included these days: clowns, circuses, and people being gay are all touchy topics. I'm not even sure I can say "touchy" anymore. Heaven knows, it's been a long time since I've called that little pink square I used to edit and erase my scratched lines of pencil poetry a "rubber," as office supply erasers used to be called. Nudge-nudge, wink-wink. Or, in Michael Scott parlance, "That's what she said." In our hypersexualized culture, the hot topics just keep getting hotter. Evidently cultural climate change is a real thing too.

WE'VE BEEN LIED TO BY OUR LOVE SONGS

What Freud tipped into social momentum has gathered incredible speed and traveled far in the past century. Whereas marriage, sex, and having children were once a three-stranded cord binding communities together (that is to say, a commitment to marry included sex and children in the deal), these three are now untethered[1] and offered individually to us on an à la carte menu. I can have sex without getting married. I can get married without having children. I can have sex without having children. And, thanks to modern fertility technology, I can have children without having sex. It's a relational and sexual buffet, and it's all you can eat.[2]

Despite all that's on offer, we're still starved for love. Research anthropologist and chief scientific advisor to the online dating site Match.com, Helen Fisher agrees we're confusing sex with relationship. After interviewing thousands of Americans and analyzing data from hundreds of thousands of dating profiles, she's come to similar conclusions: the Western world is romantic, meaning we're looking for intimacy and longing for fulfilling sex. And yet the one thing we struggle with is relational *attachment*. We seek out sex, thinking it will quench our thirst for intimacy, but then we neglect to do the work of relationship and instead let those connections fade away as we seek our next outlet for fulfillment. It's like drinking salt water: no matter how much we drink, we still thirst. "We celebrate romantic love," Fisher says of our cultural milieu, "and we do not really celebrate attachment. . . . [Our love songs] always end up with a happy ending [but] we've been lied to. . . . We want to believe it . . . but we have rose-colored glasses on."[3]

I put a pair of rose-colored glasses on once, imagining how John Lennon and Yoko Ono saw the world. The pharmacy around me—which moments before had appeared in a palette of thousands of colors—blended into a beautiful-yet-disorienting wash of pinks. Some words became hard to read on the merchandise before my eyes. The contrast was lost, and with it, my confidence in navigating the store. In a similar way our sex-crazed, post-Freudian world colors love, lust, sex, intimacy, and attachment with one broad, rose-tinted brush. Contrast is lost, and with it, our confidence in navigating the landscape of relationships. And the church is not exempt.

A CHURCH IMMERSED IN CULTURAL WATERS

Author David Foster Wallace once used an allegory to describe how sometimes the most obvious things are the ones we have the hardest time seeing:

> There are these two young fish swimming along, and they happen to meet an older fish swimming the other way, who nods at them and says, "Morning, boys, how's the water?" And the two young fish swim on for a bit, and then eventually one of them looks over at the other and goes, "What . . . is water?"[4]

To a fish, being immersed in water is thoroughly unremarkable. It's normal because it's the only thing the fish knows. And the same dynamic is at work in the church and contemporary culture—we can't see the cultural waters we're in because we experience our culture as normal and the only thing we know.

Although the church is meant to be holy and set apart in Christ, we are nevertheless immersed in the dominant cultural waters of individualism, romanticism, and sexual fulfillment. Just because we may not have noticed doesn't mean we aren't swimming in our culture's mythology. It is both naïve and dangerous to think otherwise. But even when we do notice or feel the tension between Christian values and cultural values, we tend to "baptize" the cultural values to make them acceptable.

My husband likes to tell the anecdote of a man who came to faith in a devout Catholic church and rejoiced in his baptism into a new community. Along with being taught the ways of prayer, confession, and attending mass, he was also advised that he should adopt the practice of eating fish on Fridays. His pious neighbors—thrilled by his conversion—were, however, worried when the unmistakable aroma of barbequed steak came wafting over the fence the next Friday evening.

"My friend," the neighbor challenged, "it's Friday, and that looks and smells a lot like steak."

"Ah, it's no problem," the man countered. "I am learning how things can be new creatures. I just take my basting brush and sprinkle some water on it and say, 'Beef, your new name is Fish!' See? No problem."

All too often we do the same thing. We grow up reading the same books, watching the same movies and TV shows, and listening to the same music as the culture around us. Our social habits in school, sports teams, shopping, and relationships follow the same broad cultural patterns as everyone else. As theologian James K. A. Smith astutely points out, "We are what we love," not just what we believe or know.[5] Our daily habits and rhythms (our daily liturgies, as he calls them) are a central component in shaping our imaginations and our desires. So when the dominant culture defines the good life as one of pleasure and personal fulfillment, it's all too easy to not only adopt those values but baptize that vision of the good life by putting some Bible verses on it.

One indication that Western Christians have absorbed and baptized such cultural values is reflected in today's most popular Bible verses. John 3:16, with its promise of eternal life by faith in God's Son, may top the list of one hundred most read Bible verses on Bible Gateway,[6] but the next three most loved, searched, quoted, memed, and cross-stitched verses all speak to a Christianized version of the American dream:

- "For I know the plans I have for you," declares the LORD. "Plans to prosper you and not to harm you, plans to give you hope and a future." (Jeremiah 29:11 NIV)
- And we know that in all things God works for the good of those who love him, who have been called according to his purpose. (Romans 8:28 NIV)
- I can do all things through him who strengthens me. (Philippians 4:13)

Can you see it—how the American dream's ideals of prosperity, upward mobility, and achievement are reflected in these verses? To be clear, I believe the verses themselves contain precious and eternal truths. But what is worth noting is what our *preference* for these verses—lifted from their contexts—tells us about ourselves, our values, and our expectations. Not only are we just as committed to prioritizing the good life as everyone else, we also assume we have God on our side to help.

So, too, when we begin to have conversations about men,

women, sex, and intimacy, we have to acknowledge that we're swimming in the waters of a hypersexualized society. Failing to do so increases our risk of being carried away by its currents. It's not just the "world out there" that reads sexual possibility and threat into every male-female interaction; we in the church do it too. Our default setting is to hear the language of love, desire, and intimacy as sexual. New Testament Greek may have four words for love—three of which connote deep affection (*storge*), brotherhood (*phileo*), and unconditional commitment (*agapē*)—but when it comes to men and women, our default setting is to assume we're dealing with sexual love (*eros*). When we see two women holding hands or a married woman texting with a married male friend, we—the church—jump to the same conclusions the world does: this must be *eros*, and we should panic. We are blind even to the possibility that there could be holy alternatives such as affection, friendship, kinship, and deep commitment at play.

> OUR SEX-CRAZED CULTURE TRAINS OUR MINDS TO SEE PEOPLE PRIMARILY AS SEXUAL BEINGS AND/OR POTENTIAL SEXUAL PARTNERS, RATHER THAN AS HUMAN BEINGS, POTENTIAL FRIENDS, AND MINISTRY PARTNERS.

Our sex-crazed culture trains our minds to see people primarily as sexual beings and/or potential sexual partners, rather than as human beings, potential friends, and ministry partners. This can make it difficult to find the right tone in relating to others. "I'm struggling with a porn addiction," one young man shared with me, "and it makes me afraid to be around women. I have all these scripts in my head of how men and women go from clothed to naked in less than two minutes, but I don't know how to just be with women in everyday life. What if I'm not a safe person for women to be around if I have all this stuff going on in my head?"

We may not all be struggling with these exact types of thoughts, but the anxiety about how to act around the opposite sex is one shared by men and women from the pews to the pulpit. What if sexual chemistry wrecks this? What if I can't just be "normal" around other men and women? What if the subtext of *eros* is so strong that we can never find our way to other, healthy expressions of love? Author and teacher Jen Wilkin identified a component of this dynamic as something she called "female ghosts that haunt the church," a phenomenon that deeply affects the healthy partnerships of men and women in ministry. One of the "ghosts" is the fear that paints a picture of women as sexual temptresses.[7] The church's response has been to counsel men to avoid women, and to counsel women to extreme modesty.

And it's not just women who scare us; men scare us too. I know more than one family who never let their children be with an unaccompanied man, including my husband. I understand the fear and respect their choice, but I also grieve the vote of no confidence such choices show in men, and the loss of potentially great role models our children could have. We in the church share our culture's fear of men being sexual predators. And even if not at that level of deviancy, we fear most men are endlessly at the mercy of their sex drives, which might be triggered at any time by just about anything. Get behind me, spaghetti straps of Satan!

I don't want to disregard the fact that sexual temptation is a real thing. Christians have eyes and ears and neurons and sex drives and feelings just like every other human being. We are created to respond to sexuality, which means we are also vulnerable to ensnaring lures and lies when God's good gifts are dressed up in seductive attire. God created us to appreciate beauty, to want to be known and loved, and to desire connection. No amount of Bible study and Christian accountability can (or should) remove these God-given desires. The sin lies not in having these desires but in allowing them to have the wrong place or power in our lives.

That we can experience a sexual spark with others is part of what makes us human—it is part of God's perfect and creative design for us—and yet it is this same quality that is so powerfully exploited by sexual images and content around us. We feel our sexual vulnerability keenly, like gooseflesh skin prickling in the presence of fear, and we respond by doing what we do best when we feel under threat: we strategize a safety plan and fence it all around with social caution tape and flashing warning lights. *Danger! Caution! Do not cross! Sexual peril lies beyond!*

The young man battling the porn addiction described some of the caution-tape advice he'd been given. I sympathized with his confusion. On the one hand, he was advised to eschew female fellowship and find a safe, all-male accountability group to work on dealing with temptation. "Flee from temptation! Run, Forrest, run!" they counseled. However, he also received conflicting advice from older men about dealing with the burden of his sexual desires. "Get married as soon as you can," they coached, "so you can have sex and not feel guilty about it." So, which was he to do? Run away from Christian women he found attractive until he sorted himself out? Or run toward them as fast as he could in pursuit of marriage? No wonder he felt awkward around the women in his young adult fellowship.

Caution-tape advice is doled out to Christians of every age and marital status. We accept the culture's narrow definitions of sexuality as being laced with the possibility of sex, and then we cordon it off with the Bible verses we know that fit this view. Author Dan Brennan astutely observed that the church has two main stories we tell when it comes to male-female relationships: the romance story and the danger story.[8]

> **The romance story:** Boy meets girl, they date, they kiss, they do not have sex, they marry, and incredible sex follows. She becomes his "smoking hot wife," he becomes her strong husband, and they live happily and sexually satisfied forever.
>
> **The danger story:** Boy meets girl, they date or spend time together, sex happens outside of marriage, and everything unravels.

Even though I know a hundred couples who've proved these stories untrue (couples whose true love waited and yet found marital sex difficult and painful, and others who enjoyed sex on the first date and—amazingly—no one was struck by lightning), we keep repeating them. We offer the romance story to every youth group. We shout the danger story from the rooftops. As a married woman, I've read all sorts of advice aimed at "affair-proofing" marriages, with counsel to avoid talking to, texting with, eating with, and definitely driving in the car alone with men. "Affairs don't start with sex," warned one relationship columnist, meaning it's best to stay as far away as possible from anyone or anything that could lead in that direction.

The columnist is right, of course. Affairs don't start with

sex. But the litany of boundary markers—Don't Talk To, Don't Look, Don't Touch, and Don't Engage—are neither realistic nor effective. The apostle Paul noted the same problem in taking a rules-based approach to policing sin in his letter to the Colossians: "These [rules] have indeed an appearance of wisdom," he wrote, "but they are of no value in stopping the indulgence of the flesh" (Colossians 2:23). People still have affairs and fall into sexual temptation. People still engage with pornography.

Our narrow rules might seem like a wise response, but rules alone will never be enough to keep our sinful hearts from temptation. As a result, we live in communities of men and women who are often too afraid to engage with each other, and we suffer crippling loneliness and isolation.

WHAT WE HAVE IN COMMON

The Christian world and the secular world may have different values and role models when it comes to sex and relationships, but I find it fascinating that both the Christian and the secular stories involve the same *assumptions*—that when men and women interact, the plot of the story must inevitably move toward sex. Dan Brennan put it this way:

> Freud, no doubt, would heartily endorse these two stories. But are we to settle for only Freudian sexual formation in our faith communities? As Protestants, we have to ask ourselves, why do we reduce deep, male-female intimacy in our communities to the great Freudian "sex charade?" If the church is going to present an alternative, eschatological community of brothers

and sisters bonded together as *one* in Christ, formation and friendship must suggest that Christian sexuality has *multiple* paths for men and women.[9]

Our discipleship patterns for sexual formation within the church aren't working. We have taught people to channel their sexual identity and energy into a box labeled "marriage" and then keep a tight lid on it, lest it turn into Pandora's box. We have painfully sparse language and virtually no role models for any sexual expression outside of that box. Any conversation about men and women quickly morphs into a conversation about husbands and wives ("If it's sexual, it goes in the marriage box!") or gets neutered, and we speak androgynously in broad brushstrokes about "Christian discipleship."

The scripts are too narrow, and yet our churches are full of men and women with questions about singleness and masturbation and family and friendship and belonging. We have women who wonder just how much their womanhood matters if they never get to use their uterus and breasts to nurture babies. We have single men who wonder if it is okay to serve in children's ministry or if people will regard them as creeps. We have divorcées who find, painfully and suddenly, that their married friends pull away from them because they're now seen as a threat.

Our behavior in these situations shows that we are aware of the sexuality of those around us, but in a hypersexualized world with a limited number of scripts for how men and women are to relate, we just don't respond well. We have no healthy *texts* to cope with our super-sexualized *contexts*. We are awkward. We are afraid. And much as we would like to live in spiritual communities where "there is no male and female . . . in Christ Jesus"

(Galatians 3:28), we are painfully aware that we live inescapably in male and female bodies, and that we need to relate with other male and female bodies as part of our daily life and worship. Spirituality cannot be separated from our sexuality.

The question is this: How can we envision a healthy matrix for male-female relationships, one based on a holy love for one another, as God intended? This is no doubt what we want, but when the apostle Paul warns, "There must not be even a hint of sexual immorality" (Ephesians 5:3 NIV), and there are whiffs of immorality all around, we consider it prudent to avoid other men and women in general. Just to be safe. We order caution tape by the truckload—and assign an extra-large consignment to the youth ministry.

> CULTIVATING A FEAR OF SIN IS NEVER GOING TO BE ENOUGH TO KEEP US FROM BAD CHOICES.

But it is not enough to fear sin and legislate against it. The law and its penalties have never been sufficient to bypass sin and produce righteousness. For that we need Jesus: his payment for sin and his paradigm of grace. And so, when it comes to God-honoring sexuality, cultivating a fear of sin is never going to be enough to keep us from bad choices. Nor can a community of thriving relationships grow in soil contaminated by the fear of getting it wrong. The fear of the Lord—not the fear of sin—is the beginning of wisdom (Proverbs 9:10). And John reminds us, "There is no fear in love, but perfect love casts out fear" (1 John 4:18).

If we are going to talk about sexuality and creating communities not ruled by fear, we need to start by revisiting what we mean by sexuality and wresting it back from the rigor mortis grip of Freud's cold, dead hands.

CHAPTER 2

UNASHAMED, MALE AND FEMALE

THE BIBLICAL NITTY-GRITTY ON BODIES AND SEXUALITY

y husband and I were holding hands and craning our necks toward the tiny screen of our first ultrasound. As the doppler whooshed the soundtrack of a healthy heartbeat, we followed the technician's manicured finger as she decoded the blots on the screen into neatly crossed ankles, the length of legs and spine, and a perfect profile of the twenty-week-old life being woven in my belly.

"You want to know if is boy or girl?" our Ukrainian technician asked in broken English. We nodded. "It is girl!" she announced. She printed the three-word declaration onto the pictures that we took home and gazed at with reverence—the first look at our daughter. "It is girl." And yes, she was. Yes, she is.

Three years later, a chubby finger extended in the same girl's direction. "Gi," my toddler son shouted, imploring me to praise his brilliant observation skills. "Gi, gi, gil!" Long before he had language for all the things he and his sister had in common— hazel eyes, ten fingers and ten toes, the same family name—he had language for what was different about them. He was a "boh," and she was a "gil."

SEXUALITY IN THE IMAGE OF GOD

The beginning of the Bible notes the difference between "bohs" and "gils." "So God created human beings in his own image. In the image of God he created them; male and female he created them. Then God blessed them," says Genesis 1:27–28 (NLT).

Sexuality—our maleness and femaleness—lies at the very heart of what it is to be human.[1] You were not created androgynous. From the moment of conception, when one X chromosome provided by your mother's egg paired with either an X or a Y chromosome provided by your father's sperm, your maleness or femaleness was determined. Every cell in your body has your sex imprinted in its DNA.

My daughter's femaleness was present in her first moments of cellular existence, it was visible in the first ultrasound pictures, and it was the first thing pronounced when she was born. *It's a girl!* Her sex has been a hallmark of every relationship and every interaction with society she's had since then. Every application form—for her birth certificate, social security card, passport, school, and soccer clubs—asked us to place a checkmark in one of the two little boxes next to *M* and *F*. Her gender governs every pronoun—it's *she*, not *he*; *hers*, not *his*—and affects every relationship she has. She is a daughter, not a son. She is a sister, not a brother.

From birth to death—no, from conception to all eternity!—being an image bearer of God *always* includes our sexuality. Genesis 1 tells us it is not just in our humanity that we image God but in our male-and-female humanity: "In the image of God he created them; *male and female he created them*" (Genesis 1:27 NLT, emphasis added). From the very beginning of creation, our maleness and femaleness *together* reveal the image of God. Men alone do not image God completely. Women alone do not image God completely. Both women and men together are needed to represent the wholeness and glorious complexity of our Creator.

But in that confusing period between the early years of pink and blue onesies and the married years of wifedom and husbandness—if marriage is even a part of our journeys—it's not always clear how we should acknowledge and steward our maleness and femaleness. The church has provided a fair amount of wisdom and guidelines to help Christians with the married years, but it hasn't provided nearly as much help outside of them. Much of its failure to do so in recent decades can be attributed to the influence our hypersexualized culture has had on our thinking and language.

SEXUALITY IN THE IMAGE OF FREUD

Father Freud made his mark on psychology in part with his theories on infantile sexuality and psychosexual development.

According to Freud, humans possess an instinctual libido or sexual energy that develops in five stages—oral, anal, phallic, latent, and genital. Each phase has its own erogenous zone or source of pleasure that fuels the libidinal drive. For example, the mouth would be an erogenous zone for a nursing baby in the oral stage.[2]

It is worth pausing to notice the erotic language crammed into this description of a mother feeding her baby: *libido*, *erogenous zones*, and *pleasure* don't seem like words that rightly describe breastfeeding. After nursing three children, I don't know that either my husband or I would describe breastfeeding as fundamentally erotic. I offer as Exhibit A the nursing bra, which is arguably the least sexy attire on the planet.

Breasts do have sexual function ("May her breasts satisfy you always," says the wisdom writer to young husbands in Proverbs 5:19 NIV), but they also function as providers of life-giving nutrition and comfort, as when God describes Jerusalem's metaphorical breasts providing for Israel (Isaiah 66:11). Breasts always belong to women, but breasts aren't always sexy. Breasts have a place in expressing *eros* love, but they also have a nonsexual place in expressing the unconditional, sacrificial *agape* love of a mother for her child.

Unfortunately, Freud's psychosexual legacy persists, funneling all our conversation about gender, sex, and identity into one narrow and highly eroticized view of sexuality. As a result, there's an eerily sexual overlay in a host of conversations and contexts that really should have nothing to do with sex. When it comes to our preschoolers' choice of toys, we worry about what their preferences reveal about their gender identity and orientation, instead of just seeing children at play. I've seen adults blush and fuss about kids eating popsicles or corndogs—their enthusiasm for fairground treats misconstrued as inappropriate sexual mimicry. We worry about how to explain verses describing David and Jonathan kissing goodbye (1 Samuel 20:41), or David's grieving words at his friend's funeral: "Your love for me was wonderful, more wonderful than that of women" (2 Samuel 1:26–27 NIV). Does that mean what we think it means? We are trained to see the threat or promise of future sex interwoven into any conversation about sexuality, even when we're talking about children or heroes of the faith.

However, Scripture distinguishes between sexuality as it pertains to our maleness and femaleness in the image of God, and sexuality as it is expressed genitally in sexual behavior. We need to push back against the narrow sexual scripts of the day and acknowledge that sexuality—our innate maleness and femaleness—is a much broader category, and that our genitals (and related sexual behavior) form just a part of it. Sexuality is woven into our *being*, not just expressed in our *doing*.

AN INTEGRATED VIEW OF SEXUALITY

Author Deb Hirsch described the church as being both *un*-informed and *ill*-informed when it comes to sexuality.[3] She suggested that a more integrated—and biblical—understanding might helpfully distinguish between *social sexuality* and *genital sexuality*.

Social sexuality, according to Hirsch, is composed of all the relationships in our basic social network and friendship circles. Since God created humans male and female, all our relationships are intrinsically sexual in that we relate *as men* or *as women*.

Social sexuality, then, reflects our basic human need for intimacy and connection.

Genital sexuality, on the other hand, is a much narrower expression of our sexuality, referring specifically to our longing for connection on erotic levels and ranging from a purely physical act to romance, wooing, chemistry, and so on.[4]

Within this framework distinguishing social and genital sexuality, we can say that *every* relationship we have encompasses our social sexuality, while only *some* are of a genital sexual nature. None of our relationships are, in fact, *a*sexual. In every relationship I have, I am present not just as a personality or a brain in a vat—I am present as a female. Similarly, in every relationship my husband has, he can do no other than relate as a man. He is not just a spouse; he's a husband. He's not just a child to his parents; he's a son.

> *EVERY* RELATIONSHIP WE HAVE ENCOMPASSES OUR SOCIAL SEXUALITY, WHILE ONLY *SOME* ARE OF A GENITAL SEXUAL NATURE.

He's not just a sibling; he's a brother. And he's not just a friend, but an undeniably male friend. Sexuality, then, is a far broader concept than just sex and what happens in a married couple's bedroom. "Our sexuality is deeply woven into the makeup of our being," writes Joy Beth Smith, "and, as such, it's running in the background of our system all the time, even outside of romantic encounters."[5]

Understood this way, sexuality lies at the heart of all person-to-person interaction, and its counterpart is spirituality, which encompasses our person-to-God interaction. In other words, sexuality is an expression of our longing to connect with people, and spirituality is an expression of our longing to connect with God.

"Our sexuality does not compete with our spirituality," writes Hirsch. "It completes it."[6]

At first blush, this may seem counterintuitive. The church has a long history of seeing spirituality as the solution or deterrent to any unwanted expressions of sexuality. Struggling with desire? "Either get married or pray," the trope advises. "Overcome any longing you have for sex by letting Jesus be all you need." In a nutshell, use your spirituality to cancel out your sexuality. But when we take this view, we fall straight into the dualistic thinking that has dogged the church since its first days. It's a struggle rooted in the lie that the spiritual is good and should be pursued, while the physical (the "flesh") is polluted by sin and should be spurned. "Mind over matter" is an ancient mantra.

Church history offers us an early example. Origen was a prolific theologian and biblical scholar who wanted to tutor women without raising suspicions of scandal. To make sure his sexuality did not get in the way of his devotion to the kingdom of heaven, Origen went so far as to castrate himself.[7] Sounds extreme, right? But Origen was not an outlier. He simply interpreted his faith in light of the prevailing Greek mind-set of the day, which esteemed the realm of philosophy and knowledge and despised the material realm. This deep-seated Gnosticism views the body as a problem. It's sin-ridden. It's less-than. Those who are truly spiritual and enlightened live above and beyond their bodily needs and desires.

It's actually not hard to see where this comes from. The Bible does distinguish between the life of the Spirit (*pneuma*) and the life of the flesh (*sarx*). In his letter to the churches at Galatia, the apostle Paul writes, "For the flesh desires what is contrary to the Spirit, and the Spirit what is contrary to the flesh. They are in conflict with each other" (Galatians 5:17 NIV). Jesus himself said, "If your right eye causes you to stumble, gouge it out and throw it away. It is better for you to lose one part of your body than for your whole body to be thrown into hell" (Matthew 5:29 NIV). Perhaps Origen was right to cut off his man parts, since the body appears to be a real obstacle in pursuing the life of the Spirit.

But a deeper reading of the New Testament persuades me that Jesus was not commending self-mutilation so much as using hyperbole to show how seriously we should take sin. The apostle Paul is speaking eschatologically: he is contrasting life in this present, fallen age with life in God's future kingdom. We live in the tension of having a foot (or a whole body, as it were) in both this age and the age to come. Knowing that we belong to an already-but-not-yet kingdom, and that our "real life is hidden with Christ in God" (Colossians 3:3 NLT), we are called to live our lives today as a kind of practice for our future, much like I practiced writing my future signature as a married woman while I was still engaged. Similarly, Christians need to practice behaviors now that anticipate future reality in the yet-to-be-fully-realized kingdom of God.

As embodied souls we order our lives according to the ways of the Spirit (*pneuma*), not the ways of the flesh (*sarx*), which is passing away. So when Paul says that the flesh and the Spirit are in conflict, he doesn't mean that the body is bad and the Spirit is good. He means that this present age is riddled with bad, and the age to come is good, and so we who live between the ages in Spirit-filled bodies should lean into the latter (Galatians 5:16).

Unfortunately, centuries of dualistic thinking have left their imprint, and we are quick to apply Paul's words on a much smaller scale. Instead of understanding *pneuma* and *sarx* as competing kingdoms, we understand them as competing dynamics within ourselves as individuals—*sarx* referring to the body,[8] and *pneuma* referring to the soul. Our spiritual selves are to be cultivated, we reason, and our bodily selves denied. However, the fruit of such gnostic thinking is societies that treat bodies—and the people in them—very badly. Lauren Winner, author of *Real Sex*, described it this way:

> There is a pervasive Gnosticism that continues to dog the church—the sneaking suspicion that our bodies are bad, or that they just don't matter very much. The screen on which the contemporary church works out its anxieties about our bodies is sexuality. . . .
>
> If we fear our bodies because they are undisciplined and contingent, messy and willful, we then get especially freaked out about sex, which is one of the places where our bodies are most willful and messiest. When the body becomes something to escape from, the sexual body becomes something to vilify.[9]

But we have to ask, Is this really how the Bible sees us—as spiritual people who must somehow transcend the ickiness of our bodies and our sexuality? The answer is no. The biblical view is that we are whole and integrated beings. We are ensouled bodies and embodied souls.[10] Scripture teaches that our bodies are temples—holy vessels and worship spaces (1 Corinthians 6:19). We are, as author Ann Voskamp poetically put it, "souls with skin on."

Winner insists—as do an increasing number of spiritual directors and pastors—that the anxiety we experience about bodies and sexuality "runs counter to the radical embodiment of the Christian story, which unequivocally proclaims that we were created with bodies, that God called our bodies good, that Jesus came as a body, and saved us with his body, and he and we both will be resurrected as bodies."[11]

Our bodies are not like Amazon boxes: disposable and recyclable packages transporting the really valuable contents inside. Our bodily packaging is an integral part of the gift. We need reminding that when God created men and women in bodies, he called it good. Our maleness and femaleness—wrapped in bone, muscle, nerves, sex organs, and skin—is "very good" in his sight.

GOD IN A BOD

"What about Jesus?" my two-year-old asked, perched on his potty chair and making small talk. "Did Jesus poop?"

"Yes," I answered, delighted to add some WWJD motivation to our potty-training endeavors. "Everyone poops, and the Bible tells us that Jesus was human just like us. So yes, Jesus pooped."

I will confess that I am more used to thinking about Jesus' body in the context of communion than the commode. As per Jesus' direct instructions, when taking the bread, I think of his body; when taking the wine (and by wine, I absolutely mean Welch's grape juice), I think of his blood. But in truth, it is a somewhat unfamiliar train of thought to consider that Jesus lived in a fully human body, and a fully male one at that. It is strange to think of Jesus needing his diaper changed, or being nursed, or being cheered on as he took his first steps as a toddler.

Jesus "grew in wisdom and stature," Luke tells us in his

one-line summary of Jesus' childhood (Luke 2:52 NIV). Both his character and his body grew. He grew in knowledge—learning to count, to read, to recite the Torah; and he grew physically—his body going through all the normal developmental phases between childhood and maturity. Awkward as it is to consider, this means Jesus did not get a divine hall pass to skip the teen years. Just like every other adolescent, he went through puberty, his voice deepening even as hair began sprouting in places it hadn't been before. And, along with the other hormones that trigger all those changes, Jesus was no doubt also flooded with testosterone at times, his body doing what male bodies sometimes do.

As Jesus never married (and never sinned), we know that he did not have sex. But in no way can we deny that Jesus was both fully man, in the sense of being human, and also fully male, a sexual being. He related to men and women *as a man*. Just because his sexuality was never genitally expressed does not mean that he was not fully male or that he didn't express a healthy *social sexuality*, to use the language of this chapter. Contrary to the advice of many American coming-of-age movies, Jesus didn't miss out on a vital rite of passage into adulthood because he died a virgin. He was fully male and fully an adult, a holy melding of sexuality and spirituality. His was the ultimate expression of an embodied faith.

I have no doubt that there were women (and likely men) who were deeply attracted to Jesus and made advances. I'm sure there were many mothers in Nazareth who thought Mary's boy might make an excellent match for their daughters. And Jesus wasn't blind; he experienced hunger and fatigue, and he would not have been oblivious to beautiful people or to the sparks of sexual attraction.

Deb Hirsch commented that "it is one thing to suppress sexuality; it is another to order it appropriately. A proper sexual ethic doesn't deny the fact that we are sexual beings; it develops a framework for the good expression of our good sexuality."[12] In Jesus we see a perfect example of sexuality that is stewarded rather than suppressed. Jesus didn't deny his maleness, and yet he showed us in multiple instances how a man can build intimate relationships without them becoming sexual or awkward.

Jesus was a son to his mother, a brother to his siblings, and a male friend to his disciples and followers. He was particularly close with Peter and John, the latter being so marked by his intimate friendship with Jesus that he described himself as "the one whom Jesus loved" (John 20:2). The Gospels tell us that Jesus was deeply committed to Mary, Martha, and their brother Lazarus, and spent much time with them in their home. Jesus also touched countless women in healing.

One day he pushed the boundaries even further while alone at a local watering hole with a woman whom he *knew* had a scandalous reputation. He not only asked her for a drink but also talked with her about her life and invited her to get to know him better (John 4:1–26). When his disciples returned, they were shocked to find him speaking with her. Although they didn't question out loud, "Why are you talking with her?" was frozen on their lips even as their dusty feet scuffed at the ground (John 4:27). The woman herself had evidently been just as surprised. "You are a Jew," she pointed out, "and I am a Samaritan woman. How can you ask me for a drink?" (John 4:9 NIV). In other words, Why are you making conversation with a Samaritan—and for that matter, a Samaritan woman—and asking me stuff?

Everyone in that scenario was well aware of the sexual

dynamics and taboos at play, just as they would have been when a woman "who lived a sinful life" crashed a dinner party, threw herself at Jesus' feet, kissed and bathed his feet with tears and perfume, and then wiped them with her hair. Jesus not only allowed her to do so, he defended her and pronounced her sins forgiven (Luke 7:36–50). Both of these encounters were up close and personal. In public. Undeniably sensual. Wildly intimate.

> **JESUS DID NOT WITHDRAW FROM INTIMATE RELATIONSHIPS FOR FEAR OF SEXUAL CHEMISTRY GONE AWRY.**

Jesus did not withdraw from intimate relationships for fear of sexual chemistry gone awry. He did not shame the women; he welcomed them as a brother enfolds a brokenhearted sister into his embrace. Let it not be said that intimate relationships are only for the married or those who have sex.

No.

Jesus had intimate nonerotic relationships. He had gendered nonerotic relationships. He had loving nonerotic relationships. And he calls us to live according to his example.

WHOLLY SEXUAL, WITH A HOLY SEXUALITY

Just as Jesus was a sexual being—a man—from birth, so are we. Part of God's good design for humans is that he made us male and female. Together we reflect his image, and we are called to live in a network of relationships of all different types. As men and as women we are called to intimate gendered relationships: as sons and daughters, brothers and sisters, male and female friends, moms and dads, husbands and wives—and there are appropriate loves for each of these beautiful connections.

Yes, Scripture teaches that sex is for marriage, but Scripture has so much more to say about maleness and femaleness—including our sexuality and how God designed us to long for connection with each other. If our messages about sexuality are limited to ones of abstinence before marriage and smoking-hot sex after marriage, then we've fallen prey to the idea that marriage and intimacy are really all about sex, and that even maleness and femaleness are only about genitally expressed sex.

But as we see from Scripture's witness and Jesus' incarnation, God's creation intent is broader and so much more beautiful than the narrow scripts we've been fed. Sexuality is a far bigger concept than what a husband and wife do when they're naked. Sexuality is about us, as gendered people, living with and loving the men and women around us. Just as Jesus did.

In God's first created world, Adam and Eve were naked and unashamed *all the time*, not just when they were having sex. They were also unashamed together when working in the garden, preparing meals, naming the animals, and talking with God at the end of the day. Jesus, the second Adam, invites us to live as unashamed men and women all the time, even if clothes are now de rigueur this side of Eden. This truth brought such joy and freedom to my friend Carrie when she realized it meant she doesn't need a husband and lingerie to "feel like a natural woman," as Carole King sang. She can be a whole woman—fully female—as a single person in her workplace, watching movies with friends, taking an art class, or serving on a missions trip. She can wear red lipstick for the sheer joy of celebrating being a woman.

Men and women are sexual beings, and the longings and

desires we have for connection are God-given impulses that he intended to move us toward community and relationship. Yes, sin has corrupted each and every one of our desires. But the role of the Spirit is to *restore* our desires, not extinguish them, and that includes our sexual desires.

Not all gendered interaction need be genitalized. Not all intimacy need be sexualized. Scripture gives us a multitude of role models and a richness of language to express love in community in appropriate ways. In God's family we get to live as brothers and sisters—intimate and close as men and women—without it being weird.

CHAPTER 3

BROTHERS, SISTERS, AND THE FAMILY OF GOD

SEEING FAMILY THROUGH JESUS' EYES

I got lost the first time I tried to find St. Matthew's Church. I'd been abroad for a couple of weeks, and I was sorely missing Christian community. The dean of my seminary had recommended St. Matt's. So late one Sunday afternoon the week before Christmas, I borrowed a car, printed out driving directions, and set off in an unfamiliar country with unfamiliar street signs bearing names I found unpronounceable. (I'm looking at you, Australia, with your Goondiwindis, Mudgeerabas, and Woollongongs.)

Between a handful of wrong turns and my snail's-pace

driving, it had taken more than twice the estimated time to get there, but I finally arrived, found a parking spot, and took a deep breath before opening the car door and stepping into a worship service with two hundred strangers. It had been a long time since I'd been the new person at a church, and I'd forgotten how awkward it felt. I gave a half smile to the friendly face who greeted me at the door and sank into a spot toward the back.

Minutes later we were invited to stand and sing, and as the opening chords were played, I sighed out a knot of anxiety. I recognized the song, and it was a relief to add my voice to the singing. Perhaps I wasn't such an obvious stranger here. Song by song, the feeling of kinship among these strangers grew, and when the rector stood to welcome us and give the announcements, I understood why. With characteristic Australian openness, he began, "G'day! One of my wife and I's great joys at Christmas is welcoming brothers and sisters from the family of God to celebrate Christmas tea [dinner] with us. We'd be stoked [happy] if you all could be there. We know many of you probably already have plans with the rellies [relatives], but if you don't, we're going to cook up a beauty of a meal and I reckon it'll be all the better if you joined us."

It was a fair dinkum Aussie invite, and even though I already had plans with my "rellies" for Christmas, his invitation made me feel right at home. Why? Because he'd reminded us all of who we were to him: brothers and sisters in the family of God. Not strangers, or guests, or even neighbors or friends. His invitation made church feel like a family reunion where I might meet third and fourth cousins I didn't yet know but was somehow already connected to. There's something ineffably comforting about that. This was not a room of strangers. This was a gathering of brothers and sisters. I just hadn't learned their names yet.

THE FIRST FAMILY

It was always God's plan for us to live and thrive in families. When God said, "It is not good for the man to be alone" (Genesis 2:18 NIV), he wasn't referring just to Adam's particular need for a wife. What was not good—in a world where God had thus far declared *everything* to be good—was the man's inability to fulfill God's purpose for humanity by himself. As image bearers, men and women were to keep and care for God's world and be fruitful and increase in number—tasks which one man (even a perfect one!) could not do alone. Hence the need for a strong, suitable helper (an *ezer kenegdo* in Hebrew)[1] to partner with Adam in the work God had given them to do. Once man and woman were together on the scene, God pronounced that things were not merely good but "very good" (Genesis 1:31 NIV). The twofold task for humanity—stewarding the created earth and procreating to fill the earth—could be tackled only by a two-person team.[2]

Even when the fall introduced chronic dysfunction to family relationships, God still intended to fulfill his plan for humanity through families. After the devastation of the Flood in Genesis 7, God recommissioned Noah—together with his wife, sons, and sons' wives—to the task of stewarding and filling the earth (Genesis 9:1–7). In the face of the moral decline among the next generations of humans at the Tower of Babel, God once again showed he had redemptive plans that would be accomplished through families: it would be through Abraham and his descendants that all the families of the earth would be blessed (Genesis 12:1–3).

The theme of God's purposes being accomplished through human families and ultimately including humans in his family is stitched throughout the narrative arc of Scripture. The Old Testament traces the story of the family of Abraham, Isaac, and Jacob: God rescues them from slavery in Egypt and calls Israel to be a people of his very own. That the Israelites were not just God's subjects and servants but his beloved family is hinted at throughout. "When Israel was a child, I loved him," God says, "and out of Egypt I called my son" (Hosea 11:1).

In the Old Testament, family included all those who shared common blood and a common dwelling place.[3] While the Torah had much to say about different tribes and families within Israel, at a macro level the entire nation could be considered one big, blood-bonded, land-sharing family. The intimate expression "bone of my bones, flesh of my flesh" spoken by Adam in his first poetic celebration of Eve in Genesis 2:23, was also spoken by an upstart Abimelech to his extended family: "Remember also that I am your bone and your flesh" (Judges 9:2). When all the tribes of Israel made an appeal to David, they began by saying, "Behold, we are your bone and flesh" (2 Samuel 5:1). Clearly, there were many and varied expressions of familial intimacy and unity within Israel.

No one—absolutely no one—was to be outside of familial care among God's people. Rules that seem so strange to modern ears—such as the levirate law requiring a man to marry his deceased brother's childless widow[4] and father children by her—were ways of ensuring that everyone had a family to live among and land to live on, even if tragedy struck. When David praised God for "set[ting] the lonely in families" (Psalm 68:6 NIV), he no doubt had in mind the many ways God provides for widows, aliens, and orphans—those most in need of familial love and care from the broader community. Even Jesus' genealogy bears witness to how God weaves people into his family. Israel's most famous son lists widows (Ruth, Bathsheba, and Tamar) and an alien (Rahab) among his honored ascendants (Matthew 1:2–16), and his approach to family during his earthly life challenged human mind-sets and pointed back to God's bigger view of this concept.

JESUS: MARY AND JOSEPH'S BOY

"When the time arrived that was set by God the Father, God sent his Son, born among us of a woman," writes the apostle Paul (Galatians 4:4 THE MESSAGE). In the incarnation God the Father embedded the divine family into a human family. Jesus was God's own son, yet born as the son of Mary and Joseph (Matthew 1:16; 13:55). The Gospels give a scant account of Jesus' childhood years, but we know that after the virgin birth, more children were born to Mary and Joseph as they got to "know" each other,[5] which would have meant Jesus was the oldest son—trained in carpentry, as was his dad—and the oldest brother, taking on particular responsibilities after Joseph died. I've often wondered whether the younger kids in Mary's home were ever asked, "Why can't you be more like your older brother?" Or whether they ever, in irritation, goaded Jesus: "What, so you think you're perfect or something?" I don't envy Mary trying to referee childhood spats when it was likely always patently clear who was to blame (hint: not Jesus).

We get our first inkling of something of a public squabble with his siblings shortly after Jesus begins his public ministry and ruffles some Jewish feathers. Before we get to the spat part of the story, it's important to have some background. Troubles begin when Jesus performs a miracle (shocking!) on the Sabbath (gasp!), and the Pharisees begin plotting his death (Mark 3:1–6). His audacious teaching and miracle working draw such crowds that thousands follow him out to the countryside, the quiet air punctuated by unclean spirits screeching their acknowledgement and acquiescence as they bow before him (vv. 7–12). Then Jesus appoints the twelve disciples and gives them power to do the marvelous things he had been doing (vv. 13–19). Eager to see what comes next, a crowd gathers, and his detractors speculate wildly about his identity and the source of his power (vv. 20–22). All of this sets the stage for what follows.

Every family has its etiquette rules. My very proper grandmother passed down a number of social etiquette tips to my sisters and me:

- Don't speak with your mouth full.
- Don't be mutton dressed as lamb. In other words, don't dress as someone much younger than you are. (I was worried about age-appropriate clothing for my geriatric years long before I worried about it for my teen years.)
- After a meal, don't say, "I'm full"; say, "I've done well, thank you."
- And, above all, when out in public, don't make a scene. No tantrums. No drawing attention to yourself.

I imagine if Jesus had had my grandmother, she would have been at the head of the family delegation sent to rein him in, for all of his feather-ruffling activities had put him in a scene of grandmother-horrifying proportions. "When his family heard [what was happening], they went out to seize him, for they were saying, 'He is out of his mind'" (Mark 3:21).

Just as he was winning an argument with the Pharisees about whose power, exactly, he used to cast out demons, Jesus was interrupted by a message: "Your mother and brothers are outside, seeking you" (Mark 3:32). I imagine his family tapping their feet, somewhat embarrassed to be there, hoping they can make a quick exit. And that's when Jesus makes these shocking statements:

> He answered them, "Who are my mother and my brothers?" And looking about at those who sat around him, he said, "Here are my mother and my brothers! For whoever does the will of God, he is my brother and sister and mother." (Mark 3:33–35)

With these words, Jesus radically redefines family. Those who respond to his word in obedience and faith are counted as his closest kin, now part of a community that transcends even blood ties.[6] If his mom and siblings weren't on board, they could leave without him. Jesus took the expression "blood is thicker than water" to a whole new level—namely, that his blood is thicker still. He repeatedly calls his followers to a loyalty higher than that given to their earthly families. Following him would mean a great many new things, and perhaps the greatest of these would be inclusion into a new family that would last forever: a family defined as those who called God Father.

A NEW NAME FOR GOD: FATHER

Standing barefoot next to a bush that burned with flame and yet did not turn into ash, Moses received his first instructions: head back to Egypt and tell that power-hungry Pharaoh to let God's people go. Moses also had a specific set of instructions to pass on to the Israelites: they were to pack up their goods, head out into the wilderness, and worship the God of their four-hundred-years-ago ancestors Abraham, Isaac, and Jacob. Moses anticipated the Israelites might have a follow-up question about this god giving them marching orders.

> Moses said to God, "If I come to the people of Israel and say to them, 'The God of your fathers has sent me to you,' and they ask me, 'What is his name?' what shall I say to them?"
>
> God said to Moses, "I AM WHO I AM." And he said, "Say this to the people of Israel: 'I AM has sent me to you.'" (Exodus 3:13–14)

Written in Hebrew, "I AM" is *YHWH*. It can be rendered with vowels as *Yahweh* or translated as "Jehovah,"[7] and it was the personal, covenant name God's people were to know him by. Wherever the word "LORD" is written in capital letters in our English translations, it indicates the Hebrew *YHWH* lies beneath. Many of the psalms use this personal name of God. For example, "Blessed is the nation whose God is the LORD" (Psalm 33:12). In using both "God" and "LORD," David wasn't repeating himself (like Monty Python's Department of Redundancy Department); he was making a point. All the nations around them had gods: Baal or Asherah, Chemosh or Ra. Israel's god had a name too—*YHWH*, the LORD. The Psalms became the prayer book for God's people and taught them to pray to him by this name.

Generations later, when Jesus' disciples asked him to teach

them to pray, Jesus gave them a new name for God. "Pray then like this," he said. "Our Father in heaven . . ." (Matthew 6:9). This was a remarkable shift. Before they had prayed to the One whose name was considered too holy to utter. Now they could pray as ones speaking to their Father, with all the intimacy and familiarity that relationship entailed.

My husband is addressed as "Dr. Lea" or "Mr. Lea" or "Jeremy" by most everyone, but only three little people in all the world have the right to call him "Daddy." Jesus' invitation to address God as Father is an extraordinary new privilege. From beginning to end, the New Testament speaks of how, by grace and through faith in Jesus, we join the family of God. We are invited to call him Father. All those who believe in Jesus' name are given the right to become children of God (John 1:12).

Children are usually born into a family, but Jesus explains that those who believe the gospel are "born again" (John 3) into the new family of God and adopted—having all the rights and privileges beloved heirs and children do (Romans 8). New Testament ethics are not a set of rules issued to servants; they are appeals to learn the family lifestyle. "Dear friends, now we are children of God," explains John. "All who have this hope in him purify themselves, just as he is pure" (1 John 3:2–3 NIV).

You used to be aliens and strangers, explained the apostle Paul, but because of what God has done in Christ, "you are fellow citizens with the saints and members of the household of God" (Ephesians 2:19). This letter is crammed with pointers to the big picture of life in God's new family. He prays to the Father, "from whom every family in heaven and on earth is named" (Ephesians 3:15), and frames his moral instruction in exactly the same way: "Follow God's example, therefore, as dearly loved children" (Ephesians 5:1 NIV).

Being adopted into a new family is no small thing, as I learned from a beautiful eight-year-old girl. Mariah had experienced terrible trauma as a young child but had been safely and joyfully in the care of her foster mom, Laura, for some time. One morning, Laura had Mariah dress up in fancy clothes because they were having family portraits taken. En route to the photographer, Laura pulled over at the courthouse, saying she needed to quickly drop in to collect some paperwork.

But paperwork was just a ruse for a beautiful surprise. This was Mariah's adoption day, and a crowd of fifty Mariah fans from her church and community were gathered in the hallway outside the courtroom to celebrate. "Guess what?" Laura whispered to Mariah as they entered the courthouse. "We're not here for paperwork. Today we get to be forever family. It's adoption day." A family member standing a hundred yards away captured Mariah's cry of joy on video. Everyone in that building heard the squeal of a lost girl finally found. "I'm adopted! I'm adopted!" she shouted. There wasn't a dry eye in the crowd.

Mariah's joy reminds me of the joy expressed by the apostle John. Being God's child thrilled John. Although his three letters included in the Bible were likely written decades after John first joined Jesus' family, his giddy joy still bubbled over even as an octogenarian. "What marvelous love the Father has extended to us! Just look at it—we're called children of God! That's who we really are" (1 John 3:1 THE MESSAGE). I can almost picture him crying out, "I'm adopted! I'm adopted!" And there isn't a dry eye among the heavenly host either.

JESUS: OUR ULTIMATE BIG BROTHER

The author of the book of Hebrews provides some of the theological backstory to explain how Jesus enables us to address God as Father. In short: Jesus became human so he could be what we might call our "blood brother." A TV series by the same name notwithstanding, a person's blood brother is a man he has sworn to treat as if they were blood relatives. It's a whole level up from pinky swearing or pledging BFFs.

Jesus, the divine Son, had to "share in flesh and blood" (Hebrews 2:14) so he could experience all of human life—and death—with us and for us. By effectively mingling his blood with ours, he joined the human family. He became our big brother and then invited us, his brothers and sisters, to join in the relationship he has with his Father.

When Jesus invites us to share his relationship with the Father, we also enter into a new relationship with every other person who calls on that same Father. They are our siblings. Coheirs. Coconspirators. Brothers and sisters. Our relationships with other believers are not like those in a global fan club, in which we all happen to worship the same person. We have more than our love for Arsenal Football or Beyoncé in common. When we are adopted into the family of God, our relationships with one another change in a profound way. When Jesus looked around and addressed those who believed in him as his brothers and sisters, he wasn't being poetic and sentimental—he was proclaiming a new reality.

Children adopted into the

> **WHEN WE ARE ADOPTED INTO THE FAMILY OF GOD, OUR RELATIONSHIPS WITH ONE ANOTHER CHANGE IN A PROFOUND WAY.**

same family are legally and completely brothers and sisters, even if they've never met before. Feelings of attachment (or antagonism) may or may not grow with time, but it's the mutual connection to the parent that makes siblings *siblings*—whether or not they feel it. And what any good Father always hopes for, of course, is that the children whom he loves will also come to love and support one another as he does.

LIKE, *LITERALLY* FAMILY

I'm one of those people who gets grammar-nerd mugs as birthday presents. Let's just say I'm a fan of punctuation. Consider the magnitude of difference between these two sentences: "Let's eat Grandpa" and "Let's eat, Grandpa." For lack of a comma, Grandpa is a goner! I'm also a fan of using the right words. In all likelihood, this is my parents' fault. I don't think I ever asked, "Can I have a glass of milk?" without the answer being "Of course you *can*, but *may* you?" Properly speaking, the word "can" means one is *capable* of doing something. Whether one "may," or is *permitted* to do it, is a different question.

Over the years, I've learned that being a grammar nazi might make me a good editor, but it doesn't always make me a popular friend. Language changes just as cultures change, so a little linguistic flexibility is a good thing. I don't get my back up when my kids ask if they *can* have a glass of milk. They can, and they may.

But I confess my schoolmarm snark still comes out when my eldest flops into the kitchen and announces, "I'm literally dying of hunger." It makes me want to google pictures of extreme malnutrition and snap back, "No, you're not. Here's what *literally* dying of hunger looks like." The word "literally" means something is actually, factually true. What my daughter might be reaching for is a metaphor, or a figure of speech.

The Bible is full of images and poetic metaphors that describe spiritual realities. Jesus describes himself as a vine, a gate, a shepherd, a bridegroom, a path, and a light, to name just a few. The people of God are described as sheep, a vineyard, a bride. And then there is the really wild imagery of apocalyptic literature, with its four horsemen, eye-studded wheels, and multi-horned beasts. In his parables Jesus invites us to imagine ourselves variously as servants entrusted with talents, virgins keeping watch with oil lamps, sheep separated from their shepherd, and guests invited to a fancy banquet. Jesus was the king of idiom, a masterful and evocative storyteller and teacher.

Metaphors abound in the epistles too. The church is described as a temple made up of living stones, a body made up of different members, and a vine with many branches (some native, others grafted in). We are encouraged to learn lessons about the Christian life through images of a soldier preparing for battle, a farmer sowing a field, and an athlete training for a race. Each of these images is deeply instructive, firing our imaginations to consider aspects of our Christian life from various perspectives.

However, when Jesus invited us to address God as Father and to call one another brother and sister, he was not using a metaphor. Jesus began parables by saying, "the kingdom of God is like this . . . a man had a vineyard . . . " but his statements about our filial connection to God are direct and metaphor free. When we pray, we call God our Father because he is *literally* our Father. This is the spiritual reality into which union with Christ has initiated us. God is not engaging in a game of cosmic make-believe. He is not playing house and pretending to be the daddy. The apostle John was thrilled not merely because God calls us his children but because we *are* his children (1 John 3:1).

The author of the book of Hebrews takes pains to point out how this earth's spiritual structures and symbols are all intended by God to point to ultimate spiritual realities. Israel's priests prefigured Jesus' eternal priesthood (Hebrews 7–8). The pattern of the temple on earth "is a copy and shadow of what is in heaven" (Hebrews 8:5 NIV). The sacrificial system, with its bloody bulls and goats, never actually took away human sin (Hebrews 10:4) but pointed to Christ, whose death and resurrection made it possible for God to say, "I will forgive their wickedness and will remember their sins no more" (Hebrews 8:12 NIV). Abraham, David, Esther, Ruth, and all the saints of old were ultimately forgiven because of Jesus' death for their sins. The first covenant sacrifices were placeholders for their pardon. Jesus is not a metaphorical priest in a symbolic temple forgiving hypothetical sins. Everything he did was the real thing, with real effects.

What's more, the Father-Son relationship is an eternal reality and divine standard, and the family relationships we have on earth are patterned on it (Ephesians 3:15). The miracle is not that Jesus made a way for God to come down and be in our human family relationships, but that he raised us up and included us in his perfect relationship with God. This is what it is to be *in* Christ. The author of Hebrews writes, "Both the one who makes people holy and those who are made holy are of the same family. So Jesus is not ashamed to call them brothers and sisters" (Hebrews 2:11 NIV). And as he stands before God, Jesus says, "Here am I, and the children God has given me" (v. 13).

When Jesus states he is not ashamed to call us his brothers

and sisters, he's not being polite or even kind. He is making a statement about spiritual reality—the plain truth—as he sees it. Those who belong to Christ are brothers and sisters in an existential, profound, and real way. And the implications of that relationship are staggering, especially for what it means to love one another.

FAMILY LOVE

On my kitchen wall are three laminated posters, each a customized list of responsibilities for our children on any regular school day. Their lists include boxes to check for brushing their teeth, packing their backpacks, and completing whatever chores are written on the popsicle sticks they pull from the "chore jar." Some of these chores are ones they do individually, but other tasks—such as feeding the dog—are shared. And one item all three children need to check off every day is a RAK, a random act of kindness. They complain about their lists (frequently and with much rolling of eyes), bemoaning how they *have to* do all these things, but being a fan of the school of positive parenting, I like to remind them that they *get to* do all those things. After all, I'm not trying to ruin their lives but to train them to be capable and considerate adults. And practically speaking, we're a household, and stuff needs to get done. We share the fun, but we also share the work.

"Household" is exactly the word the apostle Paul uses to describe the church in his first letter to Timothy (1 Timothy 3:12). The relational framework for everything from shared meals to discipline to house rules for how we treat each other is addressed to a *family*. Almost every bit of moral instruction in the New Testament is addressed not to Christians or believers in general but to *brothers and sisters.*

The Greek word *adelphoi*,[8] a plural noun, appears over 150 times in the New Testament, and forms of the singular, *adelphos*, at least 120 times more. *Adelphos* means "brother," *adelphē* means "sister," and *adelphoi*—the plural we're considering—sometimes means "brothers" and sometimes is a gender-neutral plural catch-all referring to siblings, just as we understand *man*kind to refer to both men and women.

There are places in the New Testament where *adelphoi* means brothers in the sense of male children, such as in John 7 when Jesus' brothers (*adelphoi*) had strong opinions on whether or not he should be traveling to Jerusalem for the Feast of Tabernacles. But most uses are found in letters to the early church, where the apostles entreat believers to embrace a new way of living now that they are brothers and sisters (*adelphoi*) in God's family.

Although some older Bible versions translate *adelphoi* as "brethren" or "brothers," in most instances it should be read as including both brothers and sisters because it is an appeal to siblings—both men and women in the household of God.[9] And translating *adelphoi* as "brothers and sisters" is not just a trendy move toward gender-inclusive language.[10] The footnotes of the English Standard Version explain 135 times that where we see "brothers" in English, we could just as well read "brothers and sisters":

> The plural Greek word *adelphoi* (translated "brothers") refers to siblings in a family. In New Testament usage, depending on the context, *adelphoi* may refer either to men or to both men and women who are siblings (brothers and sisters) in God's family, the church.

Bible scholar Don Carson agrees:

There is plenty of unambiguous evidence, both in the New
Testament and outside it, that "brothers" very often meant what
we mean by "brothers and sisters." . . . This is not a flawed translation: rather, the expanded English expression is including people
who would have felt included in the Greek *adelphos* but who by
and large do not feel so included in the English "brother."[11]

The translators of the Christian Standard Bible also agree,
noting that they weren't bowing to cultural pressure to be gender-
inclusive when they translated *adelphoi* as "brothers and sisters." [12]
Rather, they did so because that translation is gender-*accurate* and
faithful to the original text.

Although I was born and raised in South Africa, I've lived
in the United States for sixteen years. As such, I listen to things
like political speeches with something of a filter—let's call it
the "authorized eavesdropper" filter. Appeals made to "fellow
Americans" don't technically include me, since I'm not a citizen
and I can't vote. But policies and conversations about life in the
United States do directly affect me as a taxpayer and permanent
resident, so when local or national issues like funding for schools
or regional wildfires are discussed, I listen in.

Over the years, I developed a similar "authorized eavesdropper" filter for much of my Bible reading. I knew I wasn't part of
the original audience, but what was said there affected me even if
it wasn't originally addressed to me. So I listened in, ready to learn,
but often felt a sense of distance—a holy form of eavesdropping, if
you will.

What a shock it was, then, to realize that in every place where the New Testament addresses *adelphoi*, it includes me directly. It was as if I'd thought God had been talking to the person just behind me all along and then realized, "Wait! You're talking to *me*?" And not just me but all the brothers and sisters around me too. The instructions for holy living are not just for first-century Christians, with me learning from their example. They are for all brothers and sisters—*all y'all*, as residents in the South might say it—in the family of God. The words of Scripture are a family briefing, and every one of us is expected to pay attention. We are not holy eavesdroppers; we are brothers and sisters. We are called to listen up, not just listen in.

The admonitions of Scripture are heavenly realities that we, as the family of God, are to put into everyday practice. We are to "love one another deeply as brothers and sisters" (Romans 12:10 CSB), which means we are to

- show one another hospitality without complaining (1 Peter 4:9);
- care for each other (Philippians 2:4);
- bear one another's burdens (Galatians 6:2);
- forgive slights (Ephesians 4:32);
- be patient with long-standing irritations (Colossians 3:13);
- help one another financially (2 Corinthians 8:13–14);
- hold one another accountable for mistakes and call each other out for wrongs so we can learn together (James 5:19–20); and
- over all these, "put on love, which binds everything together in perfect harmony" (Colossians 3:14).

All of these instructions are addressed to the *children of God*. This is the way men and women in the family of God are to be *familiar* with each other. It's close. It's comfortable. It speaks of warm relationships in which we know one another well. *This* is what it means to be family. It's the difference between the awkwardness of the love triangle in *The Empire Strikes Back* (remember Luke and Leia's longer-than-just-friends kiss?) and the clarity that comes in *Return of the Jedi* once it's revealed that Luke and Leia are actually brother and sister.[13]

"You love him, don't you?" Han Solo asks, the third member of the triangle who hasn't yet heard the news and is mentally preparing his suitor concession speech.

"Yes," Leia admits. But she is quick to clarify, "It's not like that at all. He's my brother."[14] Her love is real and deep, but it isn't the smooching kind. So the question remains: What different kinds of love are there?

THE FOUR LOVES

One of my favorite things about little kids is their creative use of language. I will never forget my eldest's puzzled brow at a barbeque as she wondered, "Does tri-tip come from dinosaurs?" Or a pronouncement from my youngest, who had obviously been paying attention to his siblings learning their shapes, when he declared a stop sign he noticed to be a "stoptagon."

There's something wonder-stripping about teaching kids that the range of words grown-ups use is far less fun, and often far less descriptive. Tri-tip, disappointingly, is just regular beef, not a prime cut of triceratops. And stop signs are just, well, stop signs. That gorgeous golden sticky stuff my son likes on his toast is not "silver-orange marmalade," but Seville orange marmalade. Language is so fresh and colorful on kids' lips.

Love is one of those words in English that has just four tiny letters but contains a huge number of ideas. The word is so common we seldom pause to marvel at its textures and colors. The way I love ice cream is substantially different from the way I love my mom, which is different from the way I love my husband, which is also different from the way I love my alma mater. As we talked about earlier, New Testament Greek has a few more words to work with for expressing love, specifically *storge, phileo, agape,* and *eros.*

Storge is a strong, heartfelt love, such as the love one has for family. It's the love that keeps parents smiling through hours of kindergarten concerts and makes protective older brothers wear muscle shirts to intimidate young suitors hoping to date their little sisters. The apostle Paul uses a compound, *philostorgos,* in the exhortation, "Love one another with brotherly affection [*philostorgos*]" (Romans 12:10).

Phileo is a companionable love, sparked by mutual interests, affection, and kindness, such as *philo*sophers love ideas and wisdom, and *phila*telists are united in their love of stamps. I love my girlfriends and my fellow word nerds with a deep *phileo* love. New Testament writers make frequent use of *phileo.* Jesus asks Peter, "Simon, son of John, do you love [*phileo*] me?" (John 21:16–17). The apostle Paul closes his letter to Titus by asking him to "greet those who love [*phileo*] us in the faith" (Titus 3:15). There is a camaraderie and warmth to the kindred love shared among the people of God.

Agape is the most famous of the loves in the Bible, being the word often used to describe the unconditional love God has for us and the word used in the most famous "love" passage, 1 Corinthians 13. *Agape* love is based not in the worthiness of the recipient but in the esteem of the love-giver. It's the love I'm called to when my children are in the worst throes of a tantrum:

I *agape* them because I'm their mother, not because they're especially lovable at that moment. *Agape* saves lives. Moreover, *agape* is the deep, covenantal love with which the Father loves us, and our *agape* love for one another is what marks us as followers of Jesus: "By this all people will know that you are my disciples, if you have love [*agape*] for one another" (John 13:35).

Eros derives its name from the Greek god of love and conveys sexual desire, physical attraction, and sensual physical love. Although it is the fourth of the famous "loves," the word *eros* isn't used in the New Testament or in the Greek translation of the Old Testament, but we know from first-century art and literature that *eros* was well known to the culture of the day. The twenty-first century is by no means the first to be sex-crazed.

Together these four Greek words for love give us more semantic range than our one English word, but New Testament scholar N. T. Wright comments that even these are not enough:

> There are not just four things called "love" . . . there are four thousand and four, or perhaps four million and four. We need a huge range of words (as, at least in urban mythology, the Inuit peoples have for different kinds of snow) to map the complex and shifting nature of what, in English, we still just call "love."[15]

Whether we have four words or four million and four, the point remains the same: the children of God are called to "love one another deeply, from the heart" (1 Peter 1:22 NIV), and the New Testament depicts an array of options and opportunities to do that. Contrary to the *eros*-saturated world in which we live, where any expression of love and intimacy is likely to be construed as erotic, Scripture gives us hundreds of mandates and motives to love one another well, without anybody needing to take off their clothes. The biblical writers simply assume that in a family of brothers and sisters we will learn to love one another in *phileo*, *storge*, and *agape* ways. Intimacy and community in a family are built on the bedrock of these things: deep affection, common interests and stories, and a deep commitment to one another, no matter what rotters they may be on any given day.

The framework for relational intimacy is built into the familial structure. Thus my modern habit of describing relationship categories as "family," "friends," or "acquaintances" needs updating, for those in the church are my siblings—some of whom I'm acquainted with, some of whom I'm not, and some of whom I count as friends. As Bible scholar Wesley Hill observes, from the New Testament onward, friendship among believers "would therefore be understood as fundamentally a relationship between spiritual kin."[16] Instead of aiming for our churches to be *friendly*, he suggests that maybe we should be aiming for them to feel *familial*.[17] It should have the feeling of the jumble of odd-bods around the Thanksgiving table who "love one another anyway," more than the feeling of a group of mates.

It is the family level of love and support that I appreciate more than anything else about our local church. My husband and I live continents away from any of our blood relatives, but we are not alone. Our church family grieved with us when we lost our first pregnancy, prayed with us through various visa and paperwork crises, threw us baby showers, and celebrated each of those babies' births. We have celebrated Christmases, birthdays, and graduation milestones with our spiritual mothers, fathers, brothers, and sisters in the church—and this is no small thing.

A close friend recently described how unexpectedly

wonderful her Thanksgiving had been: "It was the best type of family togetherness," she said, "when you're friends, but there's a deep loyalty and connection beneath that." *Yes*, I thought. *This is how I feel about the men and women in our church family.* These

relationships have been warm, trusting, close, and connected—without being awkward or sexualized. With the deep sympathy of a brother who himself has lost a little one, my husband can give a comforting hug to our friend who miscarried—without any of us sweating over how his hugging someone who is not his spouse might be the harbinger

> **INSTEAD OF AIMING FOR OUR CHURCHES TO BE *FRIENDLY*, MAYBE WE SHOULD BE AIMING FOR THEM TO FEEL *FAMILIAL*.**

of an affair. I can text a friend to arrange a playdate between our kids even as I'm emailing her husband about details of a conference we're planning together. I can invite my lesbian friend over for dinner without worrying about any signals it might send— because she's my sister, not a dating interest.

Living as brothers and sisters in Christ gives us a new perspective for relating to the men and women around us. The apostle Paul encourages us to treat older men as fathers, younger men as brothers, older women as mothers, and younger women as sisters, with absolute purity (1 Timothy 5:1–2). We need not have fear-based, sexualized patterns of avoidance and hair-trigger regulation because we have the option to choose another pattern—a familial pattern with deep, rich, life-giving ways for us to love one another with a clear conscience.

God's goal for us is a love-based, holy, warm, and vibrant community of relationships, just as brothers and sisters ought to have. One of the most outstanding examples of this I have seen is from Laura, eight-year-old Mariah's adopted mom. Laura is a single mom who has brought several traumatized children into her home for foster care, and adopted two of them. She knows a big part of her daughter's healing will include being loved by trustworthy, healthy adults—something Mariah didn't experience earlier in her life. Laura herself is a wise, well-adjusted woman, but she knows her daughter will need other healthy women and men in her life too. So Laura reached out to two of her brothers in Christ—family friends and each a husband and father to his own children—and asked them if they'd take a special interest in being there as surrogate dads in her daughter's life. These men and their families were among the throng cheering on Mariah's adoption day, and it gives me joy to see them turning up at each of Mariah's life events: her birthday parties, her sports activities, and holding a giant "We love you!" banner at her baptism. Laura may not have a husband to father Mariah, but their all-girl household has a beautiful abundance of fatherly and brotherly support. They are leaning heavily on the family of God, and it is one of the most beautiful things I've ever seen in community.

It's relationships such as these that give me glimpses of the new heavens and the new earth, and what eternal life in the family of God will be like. And these glimpses give me hope, even though the children of God don't live as one big happy family quite yet. For now, our day-to-day reality is that the larger church family is still made up of particular local family sets. I was born to two particular parents and count two particular women as my sisters. I have one husband, and we have three children for whom we have particular responsibility, and yet we all belong within this big family of God. Thus the question we need to turn to next is this: How does my earthly family fit into the bigger picture of God's family?

CHAPTER 4

WWJD, RELATIONAL SPHERES, AND VENN DIAGRAMS

WHERE THE NUCLEAR FAMILY FITS WITHIN GOD'S FAMILY

A nervous titter of laughter rippled through the room as my husband introduced the topic for his talk at our campus fellowship. Standing well over six feet, this very married man would be spending the next half hour talking about . . . being a bride. Specifically, being the bride of Christ. The college students in the audience weren't quite sure how to react. *Where is he going with this?* A couple of them looked over to me for reassurance. I had little to offer—I wasn't quite sure how to handle my husband "going bridal." I'd been in more than one Bible study that encouraged unmarried gals to reflect on "the Lord, my husband," but hearing those words on the lips of someone wearing a five o'clock shadow made me rethink the image entirely.

Being part of the family of God introduces a seemingly complicated way to think about our relationships. It connects us in a whole new network—and can make it tricky to explain exactly how we're related. Introducing family can be hard enough (ever been introduced to "Maria, your second cousin once removed's brother-in-law's niece"?), and the Christian-family dimension adds yet another layer. While it might be theologically and technically correct for my husband to introduce himself as "the husband of Bronwyn, the brother of Bronwyn, as well as the servant and brother of Christ, and also his bride," it would probably be awkward for him to lead with that at a dinner party. Our relationally multilayered communities of faith raise a new set of questions.

How is our relationship to a brother with whom we shared a bunk bed and eighteen years of family meals different from our relationship to a brother in Christ with whom we share the Lord's supper? How is our duty of care to the older women in our congregation (whom we are to treat as mothers) different from our duty of care to the mothers who gave birth to us? Plainly put, how do the earthly families we were born into fit into the big picture of the eternal family into which we were born again?

WWJD

Long before Lance Armstrong popularized silicone wristbands with his LIVESTRONG campaign, I was a Christian teen with a WWJD? bracelet. (Yes, the trend even made it to the southernmost tip of Africa.) In any given situation, we were encouraged to take a moment and ask ourselves, *What would Jesus do?*

As it turns out, asking what Jesus would do may not be an especially helpful question if you're wanting to know how to treat your family in public. The gospel of Luke recounts several conversations in which people were shocked by Jesus' words about family. One man who wanted to follow Jesus asked if he could first go and bury his father. "Let the dead bury their own dead," Jesus bluntly replied, "but you go and proclaim the kingdom of God" (Luke 9:60 NIV).

In the next verse another would-be follower pledges his commitment to Jesus, but then hedges, "First let me go back and say goodbye to my family" (v. 61). Jesus again takes a hard line: "No one who puts a hand to the plow and looks back is fit for service in the kingdom of God" (Luke 9:62 NIV). When I was growing up, leaving without saying goodbye was a social transgression on par with tracking dog poop into the house on your boots and not cleaning it up, so it's hard not to see Jesus' words as impossibly rude. Those wanting to disrespect—or even outright reject—their families could arguably find ammo in these verses to prooftext their indifference.

As noted in the last chapter, there were times Jesus himself bluntly refused to acknowledge his family as such, much less acquiesce to their demands.[1] "Who are my mother and my brothers? . . . whoever does the will of God," he insisted, as his family waited outside. I can only imagine the stilted pause as those in Jesus' hearing relayed the message to his family. If I got a report of my son behaving crazily at a social event and went to bring him home, I can't even imagine what I'd say if the dude answering the door came back and said, "Uh, your son says he's not coming . . . maybe you should just go on back to Nazareth." It is a good thing the Bible tells us Mary was a woman filled with grace. Had it been me, everyone in the valley would have heard some version of "Don't sass me, boy!" ringing in their ears.

And this wasn't the only occasion when Jesus' attitude toward his mother might have raised some eyebrows. Consider the time a woman in a crowd called out, "Blessed is the womb that bore you, and the breasts at which you nursed!" (Try that for a public compliment some time!) Once again, Jesus redirected the focus away from his birth family and toward the new family of God: "Blessed rather are those who hear the word of God and keep it!" (Luke 11:27–28).

It is worth noting what Jesus did *not* say in these encounters. He did not say that Mary wasn't his mother, nor did he deny his brothers. Rather, in each of these encounters, Jesus used the reality right in from of him (his flesh-and-blood family) to point to a more transcendent reality—the family of God he was establishing. He was not declaring an either/or situation ("either Mary's children are my siblings or my followers are"); he was describing a both/and situation ("these are my brothers, and so are everyone who believe in me"). Jesus' relationship with James provides a good example. Jesus was James's older brother by birth, but when James later became a disciple and follower, Jesus became his spiritual brother too. Both realities of brotherhood were true at the same time.

Jesus used these conversations about his earthly family as teachable moments to talk about the primacy of the family of God, and yet Scripture also gives us evidence that he honored his earthly mother from birth until his last breath.

After Jesus had been tried, whipped, stripped, and hung on the cross, soldiers gambled away the last of his clothes in full view of his mother, her sister, and Mary Magdalene. Noticing his beloved disciple John standing nearby, Jesus discharged the last of his responsibilities as eldest son. "Woman, behold, your son!" he said to Mary, and to John, "Behold, your mother!" (John 19:26–27). As the firstborn son to a widowed woman, it fell to Jesus to care for Mary in her old age. At a time when women didn't own property, and thus could not grow their own food or raise their own livestock, a widow's children were her social security. Jesus knew his time of caring for his mother as an earthly son had come to an end. His dear friend John would need to step into his sandals—a newly appointed son to comfort and provide for a newly bereaved mama.

In commending his mother to John's care, Jesus was literally practicing what he had once preached. The occasion for that particular message was one of the messy dustups between Jesus and the Pharisees, who were on yet another fault-finding mission. The impasse this time? Jesus' disciples hadn't washed their hands before eating, as the religious regulations required. The Pharisees wanted an accounting, and Jesus tallied the situation up for them smartly: they were hypocrites, carrying on about external washing as if the outside were what defiled a person. No, Jesus insisted, it's the things that come *out*—not the things that go *in*—that make a person unclean. And then he detailed a long list of those things: "evil thoughts, sexual immorality, theft, murder, adultery, coveting, wickedness, deceit, sensuality, envy, slander, pride, foolishness" (Mark 7:21–22). The Pharisees were prioritizing human traditions and legalisms and, in so doing, riding roughshod over God's intentions in his law.

"You have a fine way of rejecting the commandment of God in order to establish your tradition!" Jesus lambasted them. And then he provided a stinging example. Despite God's commands to honor one's mother and father, the Pharisees had found a spiritual loophole and were patting themselves on the back for it. The practice of corban was a way pious Jews could dedicate extra property or money to God—a "super tithe" of sorts. However, some people were taking money that should have been used to support their parents and instead pledging it as corban, thinking they would earn spiritual brownie points for their sacrifice. Jesus was incensed. "Honor your mother and father" was God's clear command; how on earth could they think offering God a tithe he hadn't asked for (and thus leaving their parents struggling) would trump that? Jesus didn't mince words, charging the Pharisees with "making void the word of God by your tradition that you have handed down" (Mark 7:13). God is *not* impressed by self-serving rules and showy acts of devotion that undermine the law of love and the family relationships we are commanded to honor.

> EVEN THE CALL TO FOLLOW JESUS—WHICH HE PRIORITIZED OVER FAMILY RELATIONSHIPS—DOESN'T MEAN WE CUT AND RUN FROM OUR FAMILIES.

Honor your father and mother, Jesus affirmed. Even the call to follow him—which he prioritized over family relationships—doesn't mean we cut and run from our families. What would Jesus do? He'd do both/and. Which means we are to honor and love our earthly family as best we can. And honor and love our spiritual family also.

MODEL FAMILIES

The New Testament epistles are unquestioningly addressed to the family and household of God, the beloved *adelphoi*. And yet several New Testament epistles also give specific instructions to the nuclear families within God's bigger household. Paul's letters to the churches at Colossae and Ephesus both contain sections sometimes referred to as "household codes." This is where Paul addresses each of the groups one would have found in a first-century household—such as slaves, masters, children, parents, wives, husbands—and teaches them how the gospel transforms each of these relationships. No matter the culture, context, or socioeconomic class in which new believers found themselves, they were called to consider how being part of the family of God changed relationships within their earthly families.

Slaves and masters were to remember they were equal in God's sight: masters humbled by the fact that the Lord is a master over us all, slaves encouraged that we all serve a God who sees our work and will reward us. What a thought—a slave rewarded as an heir (Colossians 3:24)!

Children were to obey their parents; the loving boundaries and discipline of parents are meant to instruct us into the boundaries and discipline of God. So, too, parents were reminded to encourage their children rather than exasperate them, a verse I'm sure has been favorited in many a youth group Bible memorization challenge.

Wives and husbands, likewise, were enjoined to love and respect their spouses, seeing their relationship as reflecting that of Christ and the church. Self-sacrifice and mutual service should characterize every aspect of marriage, each spouse caring for the other as they would for themselves. Reaching back to Genesis where the blueprint for marriage was first given, Paul quotes, "For this reason a man will leave his father and mother and be united to his wife, and the two will become one flesh," and then—with dizzying theological flourish—concluded that this mysterious union he'd described *is actually Christ and the church* (Ephesians 5:31–32 NIV).

In every relationship we have—from the intimacy of marriage to the relationship of citizens to oppressive kings—the Scriptures encourage us to choose behavior "as unto the Lord," for, in some way, those flesh-and-blood relationships point to eternal ones. The gospel is *practical* in its application in every sphere: God calls us to live into our identity as people belonging to his family and bearing his name, and to behave as such no matter where we go and what we do. It is precisely because we are God's children, the bride of Christ, and his coworkers in God's service that we attend diligently to the relationships with our spouses, our children, our communities, and our colleagues.

Our family relationships are meant to *model* relationships in God's kingdom, in both senses of the word. We are to be *models* in the sense of being brilliant examples to imitate: "He's a model student!" "She's a model citizen!" And we are to be *models* in the sense of being a miniature representation of the real thing, such as my daughter's ten-inch LEGO creation of the Eiffel Tower paying tribute to the majesty of the original 1,063-foot tower in Paris. In our human families we are to live out on a small scale the recognizable patterns of the bigger story the gospel tells, and we are to do so in an exemplary way.

Our allegiance to the family of God doesn't lessen our responsibilities to our earthly families. Because the stakes are higher, the bar is higher. We are called to do good to *all* people as we have opportunity, and "especially to those who belong to the family of believers" (Galatians 6:10 NIV), and then within that framework, we have *particular* responsibilities to our earthly families.

In 1 Timothy 5, the apostle Paul gives examples of how these duties of care played out in one early Christian community. After his general instruction that we are to treat all the men and women in our congregation as mothers, fathers, brothers, and sisters, Paul turns his attention to widows. Widows were especially vulnerable in the first-century, often lacking both the resources to provide for themselves and an opportunity to work. One of the first pastoral issues the early church had to deal with was caring well for their widows, a crisis that led to the appointment of a whole new category of Christian service in the role of deacons (Acts 6:1–6).

Likewise, the new church under Timothy's care had widows who needed to be treated as "mothers" and "sisters." However, Paul is clear that the first line of responsibility for a widow fell to the woman's immediate blood relatives, if she had any. Some widows were young and childless and were encouraged to remarry as they had opportunity. But if a widow was older and had children or grandchildren, she needed to remain committed to serving her family, and they in turn were responsible for her care. "Anyone who does not provide for their relatives," the apostle warned, "and especially for their own household, has denied the faith and is worse than an unbeliever" (1 Timothy 5:8 NIV). Knowing that widows with relatives would be cared for by their believing families, the rest of the church could devote themselves to providing for the widows who were truly alone (1 Timothy 5:16). Church families modeling God's priorities make sure no one is left out.

EVERYONE'S INCLUDED

I am a great lover of Venn diagrams. It's amazing how something as simple as overlapping circles can show the relationships between different ideas—and sometimes the results are both illuminating and hilarious, like this one.[2]

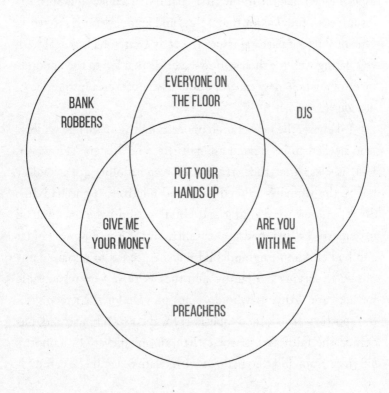

Brilliant, right? It makes me wish for a Venn diagram that maps the various familial networks in which believers find themselves, though I can't imagine how one would create it. Wesley Hill wrote, "In my experience, church community, hospitality, spiritual siblinghood, and friendship are concepts that start to overlap with one another and lose their distinctiveness, shading and blurring and becoming confused, the more you try to parse them."[3]

However, if we could diagram these relationships in the circles of a Venn diagram, one thing is clear—there would be no single dots outside of the relational spheres. There are, in truth, no "single" Christians. There might be celibate Christians, or Christians who are not married, but there are no Christians without a family. In the family of God, everyone is within a circle somehow.

We are born into families and born again into God's family. Whether we are married or unmarried, we are wed to Christ. Even if we are only children, we have siblings. Even if our parents abandoned us, we are adopted into the family of God. And no matter what our marital or occupational status, our earthly ties are interlinked with the larger spiritual family and spiritual reality the gospel has swept us into. And our daily lives are meant to embody and reflect that larger reality.

> THERE ARE, IN TRUTH, NO "SINGLE" CHRISTIANS.

In her thoughtful and helpful book *Real Sex*, Lauren Winner points out that every marital status has a particular role to play in reminding the church of ultimate realities. Marriage teaches the church what God's love looks like actualized among his people, embodying the story of God's fidelity and commitment to the community. As such, Winner wrote,

> Marriage is a gift God gives the church; he does not simply give it to the married people of the church, but to the whole church, as marriage is designed not only for the benefit of the married couple. It is also designed to tell a story to the entire church, a story about God's relationship with and saving work among us.[4]

And just as marriage is an instructive example for the whole church, Winner insisted that single Christians, too, model for the whole church what it is to ultimately depend on God:

> Single people witness to the Christian hope that the kingdom of God unfolds not principally when we nurture our nuclear families. . . . Unmarried people are asked to specialize in "creating and protecting emptiness for God," an emptiness that everyone, married or single, needs to maintain. . . . Single Christians remind the rest of us that our truest, realest, most lasting relationship is that of sibling: even husband and wife are first and foremost brother and sister. Baptismal vows are prior to wedding vows.[5]

Our earthly families have a place within the bigger family of God; we are always included in at least two circles of relationship of familial care. Christians who marry are already family in Christ before they become wedded as a new family. A man taking a "believing wife" is literally taking a *sister as his wife*, as the Greek in 1 Corinthians 9:5 reveals. The Venn diagrams keep overlapping—a sister in Christ, now a wife. Marriage doesn't cancel out that sphere of relationship; it adds a new ring (pun intended).

However, wedding vows aren't forever. They last "until death parts us," but death doesn't mean the end of the relationship. Although Jesus stated that earthly marriage doesn't continue into eternity (Matthew 22:30), Jeremy and I—and every other married couple—will still be related in heaven. We'll be brother and sister in Christ, just as we were before. So how does all this shape how we think about marriage? What's special about it? And what guidance does the gospel give us for creating healthy expectations about what Christian marriages could look like? We turn to this in the next chapter.

[PART II]

PLANNING OUR ROUTE

CHAPTER 5

IS MY SPOUSE MY SIBLING OR MY SOUL MATE?

CELEBRATING MARRIAGE FROM DIFFERENT ANGLES

One hundred and six. That's how many wedding invitations I counted when I sorted through the memento box of our first ten years in the US. Even if you don't live in a ring-by-spring campus community, the college and young adult ministry years are . . . relationally rich.

We couldn't accept all those invitations (one particularly knot-tying summer, we were invited to three weddings on the same day), but we attended as many as we could, and each has been as joyful as it has been unique. We've been to weddings with full-length sermons, and weddings that lasted less than fifteen minutes. We've been to Catholic weddings, Lutheran weddings, civil ceremonies, and decidedly nondenominational weddings. We've been to weddings with four hundred guests and twenty-four (!) bridesmaids and groomsmen, and weddings with twenty-four guests in total. There have been weddings with poetry, singing, and blessings in different languages. Weddings trimmed in peach, silver, purple, red, blue, forest green, pink, gold, and every shade in between. Weddings in cathedrals and weddings in orchards. Weddings in which the first piece of cake was politely shared, and weddings in which things went smush-face. Weddings worthy of Pinterest, and weddings cobbled together with borrowed bits, bobs, and hand-me-downs.

For all the variety in these nuptials, there have also been strong similarities. There were almost always processionals, recessionals, music, vows, and flowers. Most were also God-honoring, beautiful ceremonies, laced with reminders that in marriage we are to imitate Christ and the church in our love for each other. I love that part, just as I love the part when guests, as a community of witnesses, get to pledge support and prayer to the new couple's covenant. It is the "we will" moment, when the congregation vows to help this beloved pair keep their covenant through the for-better-and-for-worse days of their lives. It is a holy, sober moment, and I do not take it lightly.

But another distinct theme we've noted in many weddings is embedded in the speeches the couple make at the reception. Whether it's stated overtly or subtly implied, it goes something like this:

You are "the one" God intended for me.

I have waited and prayed for you.

You complete me.

Sometimes the couple use the term "soul mate," but the tone and tenor of the words often suggest that what they really mean is "sole mate"—their one and only, their grand finale in finding forever love. In marriage they celebrate finding the one intimate relationship their heart had been longing for—their lover, their heart's desire, their best friend. The couple might thank the witnesses for being there to behold their joy, but there doesn't seem to be much expectation that the community will actually be involved in their marriage. From here on, the couple has each other. They're good. They've arrived. Or, as Phoebe from *Friends* might say, they've found their "lobster." The ceremony is their way of saying, "It's okay, folks, we can take it from here."

Sentiments such as these make me deeply uneasy. When young lovers are dating, we often talk about the wisdom of "dating in community." Why, then, should we not embrace the wisdom of being "married in community"? And if the vows reinforce the myth that marriage is the culmination of all romantic hopes and longings—a ride-off-into-the-sunset moment—then how will these two fare when they don't "feel" in love? Will they conclude they've made a terrible mistake and jump ship? What tools and language do they have for seasons in which they might be lonely, or feel frustrated, or have deep conflict with

> WE OFTEN TALK ABOUT THE WISDOM OF "DATING IN COMMUNITY." WHY, THEN, SHOULD WE NOT EMBRACE THE WISDOM OF BEING "MARRIED IN COMMUNITY"?

each other? How will they cope in seasons when, due to pregnancy or illness or trauma or a job's travel demands, there is no sex?

If our earthly marriages and families model both the big picture of God's extended family and the relationship between Christ and his bride, how do we who are married handle our relationship—and sexuality—in the broader context of our community?

FORSAKING ALL OTHERS

"I haven't seen her for months," my friend said, a tremor in her voice betraying an attempt at an easy breezy tone. "Not since she got married, really. We've been in the same Bible study for years, but now they've joined a young marrieds group. They seem to be doing really well there." My friend was being generous. It was obvious she missed her newlywed friend deeply.

In our years working with young adults, Jeremy and I have seen this scenario play out dozens of times: couples marry and then vanish off the social scene, leaving their single friends a little dizzy and a lot lonely at the suddenness of the transition. Even though we were married, we counted ourselves among those sometimes "left behind," because we were the only married couple in a Bible study group of more than thirty young adults—a decision we had made deliberately. We'd been married less than two years ourselves and had been invited to a number of activities and groups populated by newlyweds. Yet, despite the appeal of a cooking club and Bible study tailored for couples just like us, we decided to forego the young-marrieds groups because, by definition, they excluded two groups we wanted to stay connected to: singles and wiser, older believers.

The church rightly honors and encourages marriage, and we do too. But after spending many years in the church as unmarried adults before we met, we'd also both felt at times that our singleness rendered us second-class citizens. Well-meaning friends described me as "waiting" and described singleness as a "season," as though life hadn't quite started because there wasn't a ring on my finger.

Jeremy and I had both experienced the pain of having close friends who, once married, seemed to have no space for us at their dinner table unless we had a plus-one. And I didn't text my newly married friends with spontaneous invitations to breakfast or late-night movies either. I figured they were probably busy having sex. I didn't realize how deeply I'd absorbed the equation: *married people + free time = having sex*. And of course, the unspoken Christian corollary was: *not married + free time = finding anything else to pass the time, while existentially waiting to have sex*. The specter of being the forty-year-old virgin haunted all my single friends, churched or not, and marriage was touted as the metaphorical Ghostbuster.

I recall one friend blushing as she recounted a brunch with some mutual girlfriends. I'd been out to eat with these friends often in the years before I was married, but no one had invited me to join in on this occasion. "We thought you'd be . . . well, you know. . . . " my friend stammered. "I . . . just didn't want to . . . interrupt anything." As it turned out, I'd spent that morning cleaning the apartment. I'd have thrown in the proverbial towel in a heartbeat in exchange for a mimosa. But I knew what she was saying: I was married now, and with all that married-awesomeness-and-fulfillment I apparently now had, she was uncertain whether I still had space in my life for my single friends.

But even as newlyweds, Jeremy and I knew we wanted to do things differently. We took the community-witness part of our vows seriously. We wanted to make sure we left space to affirm and celebrate all our relationships, with both single and married friends. When we moved to the US, we chose the Roaring 20s—a local fellowship of young adults—as our place to grow and serve.[1] We never, ever wanted to say to a single friend, "Sorry, I can't invite you. It's a couples thing." We didn't want anyone to not have a place to go for lunch, or in turn, not be called with info about a last-minute get-together because their friends "didn't want to interrupt anything."

To this day, we frequently welcome guests to our dinner table, whether they come in a pack of six, in twos, or solo. We invite families from school, neighbors, couples, and a whole lot of single friends. The wedding vow we made to "forsake all others" means sexual fidelity with each other—I will have no lovers apart from my husband, and he will have no lovers apart from me. But our vows were never meant to be a rejection of our need for, or our responsibilities to, our community. Marriage is the most intimate of all human relationships, but it was never intended to be our only or our ultimate intimate relationship. As we discovered in the Roaring 20s and still experience today, our community needs us to engage in the network of relationships around us. And we need them too.

THERE IS NO SUPER-WIFE; THERE IS NO SUPER-HUSBAND

In the past few years, we've had the joy of welcoming a number of young men and women into our home. Some have been regular dinner companions, others have lived with us for weeks or months at a time. A couple of the young adults who stayed with us were engaged and would be marrying the person of their dreams as soon as they left us. We got to see them in process in the weeks before their weddings: joy and stress and nerves and excitement all bundled up in their preparations. They shared some of their hopes and expectations for the future: the backpacking and travel they hoped to do, the career adventures they imagined would lie ahead, the sweetness of not having to say goodbye anymore. They imagined date nights for years to come, lots and lots of great sex, and perhaps some Christmases when they wouldn't be with his or her parents but could create their own family traditions. In short, it was their version of meeting "the one," of "knowing" it was meant to be, with some "happily ever after" as the ultimate dream. And of course, in some ways, I hoped that for them too.

But what I have tried to share with young lovers—both in writing and in our mentoring relationships—is that their vision of marriage will need to broaden internally (marriage itself is more complex and beautiful than having a date for life) and broaden externally (marriage exists within the context of relationships with others). One of the deep lies of the romanticized, lots-of-sex vision of marriage is that it is wholly fulfilling. The truth is that marriage can be dangerously isolating—cutting us off from others if we're not careful, and placing an impossibly heavy burden on one person to fulfill all our relational needs. There is no such thing as a super-wife or a super-husband who can meet a spouse's every relational need.

Although I didn't fully buy into the super-husband idea when Jeremy and I were engaged, I did have one fantasy. I always imagined that I would be one of those old ladies who would be dancing wrinkled cheek to wrinkled cheek with my husband when we were attending weddings in our eighties. That dream died early on when I realized that the man who was soon to be my husband was definitely of the sit-at-the-table-and-people-watch variety of wedding guest, not the bust-a-move-on-the-dance-floor ilk. There was no dancing at our wedding, and maybe once in every dozen wedding receptions I get him to shuffle awkwardly with me on the dance floor. Usually it's when the DJ calls all the married couples out and then dismisses them in order of marital seniority—the newest marriages leaving first, then the two-, five-, ten-, and twenty-year marriages, until only the couple with the longest-standing marriage is left and celebrated with a cheer. With every additional year we've been married, Jeremy's mandatory shuffle time gets longer. Maybe by the time we hit our fortieth anniversary, we'll dance our way through an entire song at a wedding. In the meantime, I have greatly sharpened my sedentary people-watching skills.

So I began my marriage knowing that if I wanted to dance, I was going to need people other than my husband to dance with. Line dancing. Or dancing with girlfriends. Or Zumba. Something. These days, our children know that if the moment calls for a dance party, Mom is the parent to pull onto the carpet.

On the other hand I think my husband dreamed of a dance-indifferent wife who would brave the wild frontiers with him, sporting nothing but a map, a pup tent, and a generous dollop of outback bravado. "You can't marry a woman who doesn't own her own sleeping bag!" his best friend had protested when Jeremy first told him he was taking his new girlfriend camping. "Sure I can" he responded, deliberately misunderstanding. "I have two." And so we went camping, and we still camp. But if he wants to do the Bear Grylls versions of those trips and compete with the grizzlies for salmon and shelter, he needs to phone a friend, because I am not the girl for that particular adventure. Two words: Flushing. Toilets.

I need friends who read fiction and who will text to tell me which book kept them up reading until 2:00 a.m. My husband needs friends who will watch (and re-watch) every second of the SpaceX launches. (He finds my enthusiasm for SpaceX underwhelming, to say the least.) I am part of a writing community, I volunteer in our kids' school, and I have ministry interests and opportunities that are distinct from my husband's. He leads a Boy Scout troop, has mentored high school kids in a robotics program, and on the weekends he likes to feed fancy food to large groups of people. Smoked sides of pork and double batches of chocolate croissants are his specialties. And yes, he'd love to make some for you too.

I had imagined my marriage being full of dancing and books and ministry and conversation, and it is. But imagine if I'd expected all those needs to be met by just one person. By one who doesn't love dancing, or hours and hours of talking, or the same books. My husband is a wonderful, smart, kind man, and—patient saint that he is—he loves me deeply and sacrificially. But even if he devoted himself to my interests and dreams as a full-time job, I don't think he could possibly fake an interest in a conversation about the Enneagram. And God is my witness that I have tried, but I just cannot—*cannot!*—get excited about election statistics. To have placed *all* my needs for spiritual nourishment, emotional connection, social engagement, and physical activity at his feet would be too much for him, or any one human being, to bear. And, Lord knows, I cannot give him the hours of introverted silence he needs, or the 1:00 a.m. conversation about technology he craves, no matter how hard I try.

This is the intolerable burden of the you-complete-me lie: the unspoken expectation that one person will meet all my needs, and that in a spouse I've found both the best friend to check all the boxes of my friendship needs and the lover responsible for keeping my proverbial love tank full at all times. Again, no one person can do this.

The tragedy comes when, several years into marriage, a couple discovers that they couldn't and didn't meet all of each other's needs and concludes that they are *incompatible* or have *grown apart*. Having come into marriage surrounded by the expectation that tailor-made compatibility, closeness, and connection are the glue in marriage, they're not sure they can make it work any longer.

"I just don't love you anymore," are words no one ever wants to hear from a spouse. The devastating subtext is "I'm hurting and feel unfulfilled. You didn't fulfill me. You didn't complete me." But how could a spouse possibly meet all those expectations? My suspicion is that, more often than not, it's not that the two people are incompatible with each other, so much as their expectations of marriage are incompatible with reality. Much like my son's inventions made of LEGO, Scotch tape, and paper, designed to "catch the bad guys and convert all their weapons into solar energy," the you-complete-me ideal—wonderful as it sounds—just doesn't work in real life.

EXPECTATIONS: SETTLING OR SETTING?

So if a spouse is not an all-in-one silver bullet to meet every relational need, what is a reasonable set of expectations when it comes to marriage? And what does Scripture give us in exhortation and examples?

Song of Songs and the New Testament husband-wife passages are the familiar go-to places for instruction. From Song of Songs we learn that the sexual desire and embodied, erotic love in marriage are God-given and beautiful, deserving of poetry and passion. In the eyes of a lover, even a full set of teeth are worthy of praise: "Your teeth are like a flock of sheep. . . . not one of them is missing," he sings to his beloved (Song of Songs 6:6 NIV).

The husband-wife passages in Ephesians and Colossians form the backbone of our understanding of marriage in God's larger scheme of things: marriage is a model for Christ's relationship with the church, characterized by sacrificial love, submission, mutual flourishing, and a mysterious one-flesh union. Love and respect, we learn, are the hallmarks of how husbands and wives are to live. Got questions about marriage? These are the go-to, bookmarked texts for any marital issues that might come up.

I came into marriage expecting that, in the bedroom, I would finally get to awaken the desires that the daughters of Jerusalem had told us to keep a tight rein on until the time was right (Song of Songs 8:4). And when we weren't doing the Song of Songs thing, I expected—according to the model of marriage I'd been taught—that our life would go along fairly agreeably, with him loving me, and me respecting him, and if we got stuck in a decision, well, he would decide. We'd heard Ephesians 5 read at enough weddings to think we knew what the Bible had to say about love and marriage.

It was a terrible shock, then, to find myself with my face buried in my pillow a few weeks after we were married, sobbing until my throat burned and invisible bands tightened around my head. My new husband was gone, the front door slammed behind him. He needed the calm night air to speak peace to his boiling frustration with me. We were stuck. I was trying to respect. He was trying to love. And neither of us was feeling like Song of Songs would be helpful on this occasion.

My tears dripped onto the page opened to Colossians 3 and its words to the married. I pored over the verses, hoping I could find the fine print between the lines to help us out of the deadlock. My eyes fell to the left side of the page, earlier in the same chapter: "Clothe yourselves with compassion, kindness, humility, gentleness and patience," it read. "Bear with each other and forgive one another if any of you has a grievance against someone. Forgive as the Lord forgave you" (Colossians 3:12–13 NIV). There it was: the specific instruction I needed for my marital crisis—but in a passage on general Christian living rather than a passage on marriage.

Bear with each other. These words have become a lifeline for me, both in marriage and in parenting. The instruction to bear with one another as believers in God's family presumes there will be irritations, mismatches, and weaknesses that—like burrs in hiking socks—may never be resolved with marriage seminars and communication skills. We may spend our whole lives working on taming our sinful habits, but our best efforts this side of glory can only ever have us be "better" than we were before, not perfect. Loving other sinful people will always require us to bear with their weaknesses, even as they bear with ours. By God's grace, I'm much less likely to lose my temper now than I was twenty years ago, but anger still flares up in me occasionally, and it is a weakness our marriage must bear. "Forgive us our sins," Jesus taught us to pray, "as we have forgiven those who sin against us" (Matthew 6:12 NLT). I hadn't known that those prayers for everyday discipleship would also be among my most-prayed prayers for my marriage.

Marriage is not governed by a separate set of relational rules and principles. The instructions Scripture gives us for living in community and loving other people apply to marriage in every way. We cannot read Colossians and think that chapter three applies only to church life, while the later verses apply only to households. No. Chapter three applies to every aspect of our relationships as Christians, with the later verses giving details to specific relationships. We cannot think that Jesus' sole teaching on marriage was limited to his instruction on divorce and remarriage (Mark 10:1–12) and his endorsement of drinking good wine at wedding feasts (John 2:1–11). We cannot forget that Jesus spoke at length about how we should love one another self-sacrificially (John 15:12) and treat others as we would like to be treated (Matthew 7:12)—admonitions that need to be lived out far more frequently in the everyday rhythms of marriage. All our interactions—and marriage falls squarely in the middle of this— need to be governed by Scripture's broad relational mandates on loving one another well.

LOVE YOUR SPOUSE AS YOUR NEIGHBOR

When thinking through our expectations of marriage, we need to be willing to love our spouse as a neighbor, which is to say we must love him or her as we love ourselves (Mark 12:31). Paired with the instruction to love God, Jesus called these the greatest commandments. The call to love my husband is not a separate category of love; it is a relationally specific application of the great commandment to love my neighbor. My husband is my neighbor. Your wife is your neighbor. Consider some of the practical ways in which we love our neighbors: hospitality, offering help, friendliness when we cross paths, caring for them when they're hurting and needy (Luke 10:27–37). At the very least, we should practice all of these expressions of neighbor love with our spouse.

I'll admit this is harder than it sounds. Neighbors can be annoying. We've had college-aged neighbors who hosted parties until 2:00 a.m. many weekends. One memorable night around 11:00 p.m., just as I was getting into bed and wondering how we'd sleep with the whomp-whomp-whomp of the bass pounding next door, our bedroom window broke with a deafening crack. A half-full beer can had been sent sailing over the fence by a panicked underage drinker when the cops drove past. It was a challenge to be neighborly the next morning as we picked our way through the broken glass and red plastic cups to clean up. But we'd been trying to extend hospitality and show Christian witness to these students, and so, even though I was tired, seven months pregnant, and my bedroom smelled like Oktoberfest, it wasn't the time to lecture, shame, or grandstand.

How often, though, do I fail to afford my family the same courtesies I extend to my neighbors? How often am I a dragon woman yelling, *"Put on your shoes,"* and *"For the love, get off your phone,"* as we exit the house for school or church, only to suddenly plaster on my kind-neighbor face and recover my polite-neighbor tone of voice as soon as we are in the public eye? And I'm guessing I'm not the only one who struggles with this. Most of us manage to restrain our sarcasm in work meetings or keep our cool with the frustrating clerk at the store, but we let our tongues vent their scalding wrath when we're at home. We patiently engage and solve problems in a classroom or office but withdraw in stony silence when there's conflict with our families.

Some might say that letting loose at home is okay because

home is where we should get to be ourselves, the place where we can let it all hang out. But our true selves—even at home, especially at home—should always be working toward loving our neighbor. Our neighbor—even our spouse, especially our spouse—should not have to deal with our unrestrained, least-redeemed selves wallowing in our worst behavior because we *just can't even*.[2] In marriage we are committing to be a lifelong neighbor to our spouse, which means at minimum we need to *try to be nice*. The ways of civility, everyday courtesy, and kindness go a long way toward establishing a climate-controlled atmosphere at home. Extreme angry heat, and extreme frosty chills in our demeanor, with wild swings in between, make everyone grumpy.

LOVE YOUR SPOUSE AS YOUR SIBLING

In addition to loving our spouse as our neighbor, we need to love him or her as our sibling. Scripture encourages us to treat other believers as fellow children in God's family, and our spouse deserves that honor too. "Be imitators of God, as beloved children," wrote the apostle Paul (Ephesians 5:1). He then gave admonitions against sexual immorality, coarse language, and addictions, and encourages the pursuit of wisdom, good time management, the fruits of a Spirit-filled life, encouragement, and gratitude. These are to be hallmarks of every Christian life, which includes every Christian marriage. We are a family, my husband and our children and I. We are also all children of God—siblings in Christ—and our behavior toward each other as a family needs to model the character of the Greater Family to which we belong. I was confronted with this truth several years ago in one of my less-than-best-self moments.

"That's God's beloved son you are talking about," my friend warned, cutting me off mid-rant as I vented about something my husband had done. I deflated. In all my complaining to both God and my listeners of choice, I was aggrieved that anyone, much less my husband, could be treating me—a daughter of God!—this way. I felt ignored, sidelined, and very angry. My friend's words brought much-needed perspective—the man I was lambasting was not only my husband but also a son of God himself. Would I say these things about him to his mother and father? No. As much as his parents are aware of his weaknesses, they love him and are proud of him and are always hopeful for his growth and flourishing. They do not gang up on him or shame him. And neither would God.

God is my husband's parent, and God's demeanor toward my husband is one of love and instruction, not shaming and judgment. God disciplines the children he loves (Hebrews 12:6); he does not discard or judge them. I may ask God to deal with my husband, but I dare not call down imprecatory psalms on his head. Sometimes it helps me to pause and think of our marriage disagreements as sibling squabbles, with God our Father as a parent. Do I really think he will take sides here? Or is he grieved that his son and daughter are hurting? Does he long for both of us to grow into deeper maturity, exercising patience and long-suffering toward each other? These are certainly things I hope for when my children fight.

Knowing that marriage means our spouse is both our neighbor and our sibling incites some deep work to train us in the ways of kindness and consistency. This is not at odds with seeing a spouse as a lover, nor does it dilute the intensity or undermine the intimacy of marriage. If anything, everyday kindness provides a foundation and atmosphere in which romance and sex are able to thrive long term.

Some may wonder whether this view of spouse as neighbor and sibling isn't too trivial an ask. Does this mean we should "settle" for marrying anyone who's family in Christ and a neighbor? Isn't marriage supposed to be more special than that? But learning to love our spouse as a neighbor and a sibling is not the same as "settling." The terrible, existential dread so many of us have that we will marry someone who is "not our true love," and, particularly if we marry later in life, that we will not get the partner we wanted but the last-pick partner who was willing, betrays our hopelessly romantic ideals.[3] To learn to see a spouse as a partner, sibling, friend, and neighbor as well as a lover is meant to expand the possibilities, not lower the bar. A spouse is more than a lifetime sex partner, and broadening our view of marriage to include neighborliness and kinship makes space to experience the richness of all four loves in marriage.[4] This is wisdom echoed by bestselling author and vlogger John Green in his advice to young adults, "If you spend your life singularly obsessed with romantic love, you're gonna miss out on a lot of what's fun about being a person."[5]

My husband deserves my romantic and sexual love (*eros*), but we also get to love each other with the loyalty of friends (*phileo*), the unconditional love modeled between Christ and his bride (*agape*), and the affection and empathy that belong to neighbors and our broader family (*storge*). Sibling love, neighbor love, and friend love are complements—not competitors—to a fully-fledged marital love.

> SIBLING LOVE, NEIGHBOR LOVE, AND FRIEND LOVE ARE COMPLEMENTS—NOT COMPETITORS—TO A FULLY FLEDGED MARITAL LOVE.

FACING IN, FACING OUT

A trip to the library will usually find my husband and me in completely different wings of the building. With the exception of *Asterix* and *Calvin and Hobbes* cartoons, I can count on one hand the number of books both my husband and I have read and recommended. One of those rare gems is Christopher Ash's *Marriage: Sex in the Service of God*, which I pressed into his hands seconds after turning the last page. It was a paradigm-shifting read, inviting us to consider not just the how and what of marriage, but the why of it—the purpose marriage and sex serve in God's greater redemptive purposes. Why did God not just have us procreate as snails do—any partner with any partner? Or as new apples do, seasonally fruitful and not falling very far from their parent trees? Why marriage?

Ash's invitation to focus on God's redemptive purpose in marriage radically reoriented our thinking. In a world where marriage has largely become *for us* and *about us*, and we wonder how God will show up and direct our personal narrative, Scripture commends us to ask how marriage in general—and our marriage in particular—fits within and contributes to God's great narrative. The function and fruitfulness of a marriage is to be lived in the service of God, with our marriage covenant becoming a living testimony to God's covenant. In other words, ask not what God can do for your marriage, but what your marriage can do for God.

Ash's book was a whopper, both in impact and—at four hundred pages—in actual size.[6] But for all its many and excellent words, one recurring image left the deepest impression. Marriage is not best pictured as two people face-to-face, with their backs turned against the world (as the "you complete me" wedding myth suggests). Rather, marriage is best pictured as two people hand in hand and side-by-side, facing the world together. Yes, there are times for face-to-face, exclusive intimacy, but the bulk of married life—and, Ash would argue, the burden of married life—is about an intimate partnership in the service of God and his kingdom. If there is one big corrective to offer the romanticized, sexualized, individualized conception of relationships and marriage, it is this: God bids us turn outward, not inward.

Perhaps the clearest example of this comes when we have children. The fruit of the sexually intimate part of marriage is, most often, the birth of babies. What began as a private relational act results in a network of very public relationships. In sex we relate to one another with *eros* sexuality, but as parents, our *social* sexuality is at play: gendered, but not sexual. As parents, we are Mom and Dad for many more hours than we are the Lover and the Beloved. The bulk of a couple's married lives is spent not face-to-face in bed but side by side in the kitchen and living room and carpool, in the shared work raising of children. Done well, passion paves the way for partnership, which is a good thing to remember when we're on the lookout for a spouse.

LOVE MATCH

Our friend Stanford has become something of a local celebrity for his witty, wise talks on relationships, dating, and marriage. When the students in our college ministry ask starry-eyed questions about dating and finding "the one," his counsel includes asking whether they can see themselves parenting alongside this person who has caught their eye. Students are often taken aback. They'd only gotten as far as thinking about conversation topics for a first date, and Stanford throws in parenting as a yardstick? But he's consistent and insistent in his counsel on who to date (and thus who to marry): marry someone *godly*, someone you *like*, someone you can *work with*, and someone you think would make a great mother or father to your kids.

Not only does Stanford firmly believe that such relationships have the highest likelihood of supporting and being supported by a lifetime of satisfying sex (and, being a data kind of guy, he has graphs and stats to show why that's true[7]), but he also firmly believes this is the kind of beautiful vision for marriage that can flourish as God intended. "In twenty years' time, if you find yourself on the couch late at night folding laundry and trying to match socks, and you look across at the wife of your youth and think, 'There's no one I'd rather be folding socks with,' then I'd call that winning," I've often heard him say.

It's a beautiful thing to conceive of a marriage in which there is comforting togetherness even in something as mundane as folding socks. And the sock imagery actually works at multiple levels, because when I think of marriage, I think not only of a couple contentedly folding socks together but of a couple themselves as a sort of metaphorical pair of socks. After the initial love match, one is part of a pair, and even after a long day of being hard at work separately, each is still somehow keeping in step with the other. Then it is a sweet thing to be folded up together at the end of the day.

Socks, like marriage, are also part of a much bigger picture. Socks are just one item out of a closet of clothes. And marriage is one relationship in a network of love relationships. At its best, a marriage is located within a larger community of healthy relationships, and has both the depth and breadth necessary for a couple to love and partner with each other in this world.

My husband is not just my lover; he is my neighbor. He is my closest and most intimate neighbor, but he's not my only neighbor. I cannot forget that we live in a neighborhood filled with other neighbors. I am his wife, but I am his sibling too. I am his closest sibling, but not his only one. We belong to a church, a community, and a world filled with other sacred siblings.

From here we turn to the burning question raised by all this talk of spouses and other people: If we count our spouses as neighbors, siblings, and friends, how does that shape the way we relate to other neighbors, siblings, and friends? Or, to put it more plainly, can married men and women be friends with people of the opposite sex?

CHAPTER 6

CAN MEN AND WOMEN BE JUST FRIENDS?

FINDING A FRAMEWORK FOR HEALTHY ADULT FRIENDSHIPS

The subject line in the email immediately caught my attention: "Can married people be friends with the opposite sex?" In the months I'd been fielding questions from my blog readers about various aspects of dating and marriage, no one had put the question quite so baldly before. I brewed a cup of tea and clicked to read the email.

Dear Bronwyn,

My marriage has been through a rough year and we've become emotionally distant. My husband developed a friendship with a female coworker, which I initially was comfortable with as he has good, informal friendships with most of his coworkers.

As the year went on, the communication increased. At the end of last year, I realized he had a very deep emotional connection to her, and I now felt threatened by their friendship. He says that if a friendship is beneficial to his well-being and helps him to be a better person, then it should be encouraged, which I guess puts me in jealous-wife space: any cross-gender friendship feels threatening now.

I need a biblical perspective. What is a godly view of cross-gender friendships, and how should they be approached within the context of marriage?

Worried Wife

Worried Wife's concerns are not unfounded. The number of marriages wrecked by inappropriate relationships with coworkers are devastating. I've sat with far too many women and men heartbroken by betrayal. They wonder what signs they missed, what they could have done differently, what anyone could possibly do to prevent such a thing. Should they have noticed their husband laughing more brightly than usual at someone else's joke? Should they have spoken up and insisted their wife not go to that team-building day away from the office, knowing that Eric from sales—who also happens to be the local CrossFit champion—would be there?

The question underlying such questions is this: Is it safe for married men and women to have friendships? Or, as Harry says in *When Harry Met Sally*, are we to conclude that "men and women can't be friends, because the sex part always gets in the way"? Living in the world we do, where everything is spun with sexual innuendo, do chastely intended friendships even stand a chance? Or are they doomed to become awkward at best and devastating at worst?

Many have concluded that, the risks of sexual unfaithfulness being what they are, it's better not to "tempt fate." If we're married, we're advised to limit our circle of friends to ones of shared gender. A popular Christian magazine wrote an article warning against the dangers of even texting someone of the opposite sex, likening the privacy of the medium to talking with someone behind a closed bedroom door. The author went so far as to caution married people from even giving their phone number to the opposite sex. Reader, allow me to make a confession: I rolled my eyes. The advice, while well intended, was reminiscent of a paranoid parent who never wants her children to get sick and so imprisons them in a hermetically sealed house, rather than teaching the basics of hand-washing and public health. It's like saying to a teen, "people die in car accidents, so I won't teach you to drive." Not only is this no way for humans to live and thrive, but the assumptions underlying the "don't even go there" approach also raise several problems. I've identified six.

1. FORBIDDING MALE-FEMALE FRIENDSHIPS IS NOT PRACTICAL.

Perhaps there was a time when men and women could stay in completely separate social spheres, but the reality for most of us today is that men and women share classrooms, offices, projects, leadership responsibilities, and community spaces. Avoiding the other sex completely is just not possible. We would be creating rude, awkward, or even frosty work environments if we had to avoid conversation or friendship with anyone of the opposite sex.

Politicians, professors, pastors, and parents on the PTA all need to be able to develop camaraderie with one another. By definition, teamwork requires building *teams*, which in turn requires personal engagement with the personalities and talents of people around us. And a lot of the time that means at least being friendly.

2. FORBIDDING MALE-FEMALE FRIENDSHIPS MAKES IT ALMOST IMPOSSIBLE TO INCLUDE WOMEN IN MINISTRY PARTNERSHIPS.

No matter where a church stands on the question of women in leadership, all churches should be concerned about having both men and women deeply engaged in discipleship and spiritual formation. As such, there needs to be a healthy relationship among leaders, including those of the men's and women's ministries.[1] Jesus called those with whom he shared the Father's business his *friends* (John 15:15), and if we believe the Great Commission in Matthew 28 includes all Christians—male and female— then we need to learn how to be friends, or at least ministry partners, together. To say men and women can't be friends effectively excludes women from strategic kingdom participation.

> IF WE BELIEVE THE GREAT COMMISSION IN MATTHEW 28 INCLUDES ALL CHRISTIANS—MALE AND FEMALE—THEN WE NEED TO LEARN HOW TO BE FRIENDS, OR AT LEAST MINISTRY PARTNERS, TOGETHER.

3. FORBIDDING MALE-FEMALE FRIENDSHIPS ASSUMES THE WORST ABOUT BOTH MEN AND WOMEN.

If we take the line that "men and women should just stay the heck away from each other unless they're married or else they're an affair waiting to happen," we're buying into two terrible and insulting beliefs. It is neither true nor fair to treat all women as potential temptresses,[2] nor is it true or fair to treat all men as helpless victims of their sex drives.

In our early days of dating, my husband once sent me a cryptic note, saying, "behavior betrays belief." In short: what you really believe about something will come out in the way you act (regardless of what you say). We can say we have a "positive view of men" or a "positive view of women" until the cows come home, but if we continually avoid friendships with them for fear of sexual immorality, there's a fundamental lie in our bedrock beliefs. Christians should have a better story to tell of human sexuality—in its brokenness and also in its beauty— than assuming the Freudian sex-crazed narrative is right.

4. FORBIDDING MALE-FEMALE FRIENDSHIPS DOESN'T ACCOUNT FOR SAME-SEX ATTRACTION.

In this day and age, it seems naïve to think that by keeping men and women separate, sexual temptation won't be an issue. The award-winning TV show *Grace and Frankie* tells of two women who become unlikely friends after their husbands of many years leave them for each other. The premise of the show is not far-fetched: marriages break up because of sexual attraction to people of the same sex as well as the opposite sex. I've read heartbreaking, heartbroken stories from both men[3] and women[4] who, longing to be faithful to their marriage or celibacy vows, have struggled deeply with attraction to close friends of the same sex. The "just be friends with your own gender" advice made things more difficult, not easier, for them. And in ministry settings, keeping men and women separate is no guarantee that sexual abuse won't happen then either.[5] Men can groom and abuse men, and women can groom and abuse women.

Whatever we say about stewarding sexual faithfulness needs to be tender to the fact that attraction can spark in more than one direction.

5. FORBIDDING MALE-FEMALE FRIENDSHIPS TAKES AN ANEMIC VIEW OF MARRIAGE.

"I married my best friend" is a common thing to hear at weddings or read on anniversary Instagram posts. While our spouses should be our friends (and siblings, and neighbors), I worry that the "I married my best friend" sentiment reflects a dangerously idealized view that once you've met "the one," he or she will be your BFF, your über friend, your all-in-one, and meet all your social and emotional needs.[6] But as we've explored in previous chapters, a marriage isn't meant to bear that kind of load. No one person can fulfill all the relational needs we have.

Healthy marriages need communities, and communities need healthy marriages. Believers are meant to use their gifts in the service of the entire body of Christ, and each of us needs the gifts of the entire body. It would be a terrible thing if my husband was only allowed to have male friends and be my covenantal BFF; our marriage vows shouldn't deprive the women in our church from getting to know him or deprive him of learning from them. And I have some brothers in our church whom I count as dear friends; I hope I enrich their lives a fraction of the amount they enrich mine. God intended marriage to be a foundational building block to communities of men and women. If we see marriage not as a foundation but as an obstruction to relationships, we've misread the instructions.

6. FORBIDDING MALE-FEMALE FRIENDSHIPS LEAVES PEOPLE OUT.

"Church feels like a married people's club." That's a statement I hear from an increasing number of unmarried Christians who express how hard it is to be in church if you don't have a spouse. Western church culture prefers and prioritizes married couples (and their children), often leaving an increasing number of people feeling that they're on the margins of church life. For widows, those who are divorced, and the unmarried, it can be hard to find a place in which they are welcomed as trusted, empowered, fully included members of the community. For example, pastoral search teams might specify that only married candidates will be considered, and elder boards might overlook single candidates because of the "husband of but one wife" clause, thereby missing out on candidates who might be as qualified and capable as the apostle Paul himself.

Sometimes, the sleights are painfully prejudiced, as an

unmarried believer in her forties described: "Certain assumptions are made about older single people. They're weird or lack emotional intelligence; they've been dating the wrong way; or they're held back by character defects or unresolved sin."[7] I've never heard anyone express these views out loud, but I can't argue with the observation that some behavior toward unmarried believers certainly suggests that those prejudices might lurk beneath. Part of the problem of having little language for sexuality outside of marriage means we might find unmarried men and women mysteriously threatening: after all, if it's better to marry than to burn with passion,[8] does that mean the unmarried might spontaneously combust?

Discouraging and distrusting friendships between men and women makes this already lonely experience of unmarried Christians in the church that much worse. If married people treat single men and women in the church as threatening (or just unnecessary) to their marriages—that message carries throughout the whole community, and we wind up with lonelier marrieds as well as lonelier and hurting singles. And if we don't leave space for single men and women to develop warm friendships with their brothers and sisters, church will feel like a dating pool (and a sparsely stocked one, at that) rather than the family it truly is.

FIRST PRINCIPLES BEFORE FEAR

Once upon a time (in a country far, far away), I was a student in a legal ethics class. The topic under discussion was abortion rights, and my twenty-year-old Christian self was exceedingly anxious about how to be and think in that class. I did not come to any new conclusions during the lecture, but I did learn a new thing about the methods we use in moral reasoning. The gist was that ethical systems shouldn't be built on worst-case scenarios; they should be developed from first principles. In the case of abortion and reproductive rights, it was of no help to our class to start with questions such as "What if a woman is seven months pregnant and her life is at risk?" or "What if the pregnancy is the result of rape?" Rather, we needed to start with the building blocks: When does life begin? Or, more to the point, when should the law acknowledge legal personality as beginning?

Developing any set of rules based on what could go wrong isn't the right place to start. The right place to start is with the purpose and vision—first principles—of what is at issue. Once we're clear on first principles, we can tease out the implications for the harder cases. This is true for everything from the trickiest moral tangles to everyday situations, such as the rules of a kindergarten classroom or regulating traffic.

> **DEVELOPING ANY SET OF RULES BASED ON WHAT COULD GO WRONG ISN'T THE RIGHT PLACE TO START.**

If, for example, we were to legislate road rules based on the horror stories of car accidents caused by phone-distracted drivers, we might reasonably ban anyone who owned a mobile phone from getting a driver's license or buying a car. That would make roads instantly safer, wouldn't it? *Problem solved!* But the purpose of roads is to allow people to travel, and the purpose of phones is to allow people to communicate, and so the conversation about road rules necessarily needs to start there.

This start-with-first-principles method is the bedrock of ethics in God's kingdom too. Jesus said *all* the law and the prophets rested on the two essential commandments: to love God, and to love our neighbor as ourselves (Matthew 22:37–40). Everything else is developed from those first principles.

When we approach the ethics of male-female friendships by working our way back from worst-case scenarios, we approach things from the wrong end. And that's what happens when we try to govern our male-female relationships by beginning with the question "How can we avoid sexual sin?" That's framing the whole conversation around the worst-case scenario.

God has given us a framework—his first principles, if you will—to ask a better question. If we ask instead, "How can men and women live in relationship as God intended?" we are better able to find our bearings and chart a path forward. Our earthly families along with the bigger family of God provide both a matrix for us to consider how we can relate, and a strong foundation for navigating the trickier questions as they come. Central to the challenge, then, is figuring out how a "big family" mindset helps us think through our everyday category of friendship.

FRIENDSHIP BASED ON KINSHIP

Friendship is how we describe those relationships of affinity, connection, and care among the broader community of people we know. Friendship chooses from among acquaintances and invests more deeply and more personally. We recognize in a friend something that sparks interest, delight, or recognition.[9] It's our most recognizable form of *phileo* love. We might share a passion (a love of graphic novels, or ice hockey, or kayaking), or share a season of life (raise your hand if you've made friends during a college finals study session, or on the sidelines of the weekly youth soccer league matches). We might find friends among those who share a mutual goal—such as training for a triathlon, working together against human trafficking, or teaming up with Leslie Knope of *Parks and Rec* to turn a pit into a park. Or, perhaps like Jim and Pam in *The Office*, we befriend a colleague to survive in the same ridiculous work environment. However it happens, friendship acknowledges an affinity that recategorizes a person into a different relational tier—he or she is no longer just one person among a sea of acquaintances, but a person of particular interest.

Everyone on earth can experience both friendship and family, but those who share a common faith in Christ have a spiritual connection that necessarily transforms their experience. Becoming a Christian is a fundamental change of "status"—it affects every relationship. When I got married, it wasn't only my relationship with my husband that changed. Marriage changed my relationship with my parents (a new name and next of kin), the government (a new tax status), my health-care provider (a new set of conversations with my ob/gyn), and my social network (among other things, I wouldn't be interested in dating anyone). A change in one significant relationship had a ripple effect into all my other relationships.

So, too, being united to Jesus ripples into every relationship we have, fundamentally changing who we are vis-à-vis one another. Our primary matrix for relating to other Christians is no longer figuring out whether they're "acquaintances" or "friends," but rather knowing they are brothers and sisters and moving from there. The kindred spirits we look for in friendship now draw from a deeper connection of kinship. When it comes to how believers should treat male and female friends, we have our first principles—treat them as brothers and sisters.

Let's circle back to the beginning of this chapter and the letter from Worried Wife. Here is my reply:

I'm sorry to hear things have been tough. Marriage can be so hard. And yes, there are some seasons that are better than others, but when you realize you're getting distant and there are obstacles between you, then it's important to be brave and talk about those things.

I don't know that there is one "biblical" perspective on male-female friendships when you are married: this is a wisdom-and-love issue, to be sorted out contextually, rather than a right-and-wrong issue that can be sorted out with a proof text. For sure, mature adulthood calls us to be in healthy relationships with both men and women—at work, socially, and in worship. I have men I consider friends, and my husband has women he considers friends. But, as you already know, not all friendships are equal.

The guideline in Scripture for healthy relationships across gender lines that comes to mind is 1 Timothy 5:1–2, "Treat younger men as brothers, older women as mothers, and younger women as sisters, with absolute purity" (NIV). As mature believers, we are called to have relationships with both men and women— but we need to make sure these remain brother- and sister-like in their tone and purity. I'm not sure the right question is, "Should we have this friend or not?" Friend is not a helpful category for discernment. The question is, are we behaving as siblings would?

Bronwyn

It seemed to me that Worried Wife's husband was possibly being more flirtatious than filial in his attentions to his coworker, and I worried for this couple. There was a limit to the help I could offer, being so far removed from their situation. What their marriage likely needed was feedback from people closer to them, who could help this husband assess the danger levels.

LITMUS TESTS FOR LOVE

One of the telltale signs of my dad's lifelong love of chemistry was that he kept litmus tests in his desk. These little strips of paper—so beautifully color coded in shades of red and blue—could be dipped into most any liquid, and the strip would change color to indicate how acidic or alkaline that liquid was. Usually only two types of people keep litmus tests: people who own swimming pools and need to make sure their pool water doesn't turn Hulk-green, and people who run classroom chemistry experiments. And then there was my dad, who let us turn the house into a chemistry lab. We tested the pH of our soda, our bathwater, our tears, our saliva, and the cat's saliva too. Watching the reds and oranges develop gave us instant feedback on how dangerous an acid we might be dealing with.

We have a similar tool for being wise with our male-female friendships. One primary litmus test for determining the potential danger level of a friendship is getting feedback from our community, and especially our spouse. If Worried Wife felt that her husband's attachment to her was waning and his attachment to another friend was growing, her husband should have seen that as a bright-red warning light. Just as a high acidity level in a swimming pool is a signal to stop adding one chemical and balance it out by adding another, we sometimes need to make relational adjustments—giving less attention to one relationship and more attention to another—once we've gotten a reading on where things are at.

This is not to say that we as spouses are at the mercy of our partner's insecurities. There certainly are partners who make controlling, manipulative demands,[10] and the broader communities around us can help be a litmus test for diagnosing that kind of unhealth. But in a relationship with healthier boundaries, part of our calling in a marriage covenant is doing everything we can to love our spouse. Responding sensitively to his or her needs and hurts is part of that. What Worried Wife was saying to her husband wasn't so much "I don't want you to be close to her," but "I want you to be close to me!" If a friendship is an obstacle to a married couple being close, that's not a great sign.

Friends who are functioning as healthy siblings in a relationship want their brothers and sisters to have thriving marriages. Our friends should be cheerleaders for our marriages, not competitors (or predators!) to them. It is not enough for us to be a friend to an individual; we need to be a friend to their marriage as well. I remember with gratitude a phone call from a friend with whom I'd spent the day venting my marital frustrations. My friend showed herself a friend to both me and to my marriage when she picked up the phone later that evening. She acknowledged that, yes, I was angry and hurt, but she also held up a mirror to my behavior. Friendship meant more than automatically taking my side and jumping on the bandwagon about how exasperating husbands could be. Friends don't add fuel to dangerous fires. Friendship—the kind of friendship that revealed her to be a sister in Christ to me *and* to my husband—meant she gently rebuked me for sinning in my anger. I could be mad, but I wasn't to be mean.

Years later, when that same friend went through a marital

crisis of her own, I remembered her example. The reports of what her husband was doing were damning, and often it was all I could do not to yell, "I think you should just leave him already!" when we talked on the phone. But to be a soul-sister friend to her, and a sister to her husband (my brother in Christ), I needed to bite my tongue and be a friend to their marriage.

When Worried Wife questioned her husband about his female friend, he responded that the friendship was beneficial to his well-being and helped him to be a better person. But he was wrong. The friendship with his colleague was *not* making him a better person if it made him a less attentive husband who was oblivious (or worse, unconcerned) about the growing emotional distance with his wife.

However, not all friendships are like that. I can think of a dozen examples of friendships with brothers and sisters who support my marriage. These relationships are characterized by the integrity, communication, and community that healthy sibling relationships need to survive. We practice honesty (with ourselves and one another), confession, and invite one another to speak up if one of us sees something unhealthy.

An example is our small group from church. We are a hodge-podge collection ranging in age from preschoolers to grandparents in their seventies. Our number includes single moms, widows, unmarried working professionals, some empty-nesters, and a few like us who fit in the nuclear family category. We eat and pray together, and while we sometimes break up into smaller groups (and sometimes do so by gender), it is also completely acceptable for my husband to offer a hug to our unmarried college grad friend when she's had a rough week, or for me to share a book I've loved with another of the married men in our group. We're siblings first, and that familial framework both sets and keeps the tone appropriate.

In our respective work, my husband and I both have female and male coworkers. I sit in meetings and share ministry responsibilities with men I not only respect but also enjoy and call friends. In truth, this book would not have come to be without many long conversations among myself, Dan, and Stanford—both friends and brothers—as we planned retreats for our college ministry over lunches, texts, and emails.

My husband, on the other hand, works in a male-dominated profession and is aware of the need to be a brotherly type of coworker who advocates for women's voices to be heard. He's never shared a hotel room at a conference with a female coworker, but if they need to carpool to meetings, they do so because it's important that women be at these meetings. When the end of the year rolls around, he and I host the office Christmas party for all his coworkers and their significant others.

The key to maintaining good relationships in friendship and at work, while also being wise and respectful of one another, is keeping communication lines open. Among other things, that means we share passwords, and we won't be sworn to secrecy from each other if anyone makes personal disclosures in our individual conversations. I don't show my husband all my texts and emails (he'd be bored to tears if I tried to include him in all my group conversations), but I'm always willing to. He has access to my email and social media accounts and could read them if he wanted, and I have the same permissions to his inbox and browser history.

Socially, our family is friends with a couple of other families, and within that bigger group are a network of interlaced friendships. Our daughter and sons have growing friendships with the boys and girls as well as the adult men and women around them, and we celebrate that. I regularly drink tea and walk with two of the wives, but when we all get together, I play word games with one of the husbands because he and I are insufferable Scrabble nerds and nobody else usually wants to play with us. One of the wives and two of the husbands in this same group of friends are fans of craft beer, and since I am not, I bow out of microbrewery expeditions. These friendships are life-giving, not awkward for our marriages; they are gendered without being sexual. I see these men as my brothers, not potential sexual partners. Any hint of the latter would make it weird for all of us.

TOWARD HOSPITALITY AND HOLINESS

It is my conviction that not only *can* women and men be friends but we *should* be. There are many ways Scripture challenges us to shape our thinking and behavior to be more consistent with the life to come, because we are people who have been given an eternal life that has already begun in us. We are in the process of becoming more like Jesus, and one day we will see him face-to-face and ultimately be like him. "All who have this hope in him purify themselves," insisted the apostle John (1 John 3:3 NIV). We cultivate patience, love, kindness, gentleness, and all those other good virtues because we are unswervingly moving toward an eternal future characterized by those things. In the same way, knowing that we will share eternity together as brothers and sisters in Christ, we practice loving one another deeply now (1 Peter 1:22). Our relationships should be so genuine and winsome that the *world* recognizes we're Jesus-people (John 13:35). Loving just our earthly family is far too small a vision. It's got to go wider. We need to love our friends as family too. The church loving one another as family is integral to our gospel witness to the world.

This conviction lies at the heart of the call to Christian hospitality, which is the lived-out habit of welcoming others into the life we have in Christ. No matter what our marital status, we are called to hospitality. Wesley Hill sees this exercised and expressed in some surprisingly particular ways among the married:

> Marriage isn't for self-indulgence, nor does it authorize a cozy respite from community. It is, rather, for receiving love from God and channeling it to others. In the first place, then, Christian spouses will look for ways to resist the easy embrace of contraception, the habit of viewing their love as a license to hold themselves back from hospitality, and all the ways that they are tempted to retreat from the needs of widows, divorcés, and other single people.[11]

Having children is a spectacularly effective crash course in teaching a couple to be other-person centered. Working together to attend to the bodily, emotional, social, and spiritual needs of the tiny people God puts into our lives is acute hospitality training. It's neighborliness boot camp, and there is no bell to ring to bow out. Hill is right when he says that "children are the first strangers we welcome," and that those skills of patience, empathy, and generosity are easily transferable. These can (and should) be used to welcome others.

Jeremy and I are trying to embody these values in our home. We want to be a family who is open to relationships with the men and women we encounter out there in the world. When we bought a play structure, we put it in the front yard so the neighborhood kids would be able to play in it too. Our front door mat bears words of both welcome and warning: "Just so you know, there's like a lot of kids in here." There are. And there are a lot of adults too. We host game nights and invite people over to make ice cream with us. We resist the temptation to turn our guest room into a dumping ground for odds and ends because we want it to be ready at a moment's notice for anyone who needs a place to crash. We want our kids to know they can always invite someone home for a meal. We're trying to live a life that says, no matter who you are—male or female—we're open to a relationship with you. For us, hospitality is more than a setting on our extraversion/introversion scale; it's a kingdom value.

Author and pastor Ty Grigg suggested there's even more to be said for hospitality. When it comes to discerning rules about friendships between men and women, he argued that "boundaries between genders should be informed by hospitality rather than legalism."[12] Rather than creating guidelines based on fear and worst-case scenarios, he encouraged us to think about seeking ways to create safe, welcoming spaces:

> Hospitality is concerned with the physical and emotional elements that make a space safe. The focus is not on the host's needs but on what makes the guest feel safe and at ease. . . . For example, I would not meet another woman in my bedroom, because that space is dripping with the intimacy of life with my wife and the privacy of where I sleep at night. Nobody would feel comfortable meeting in there. I would not have a candlelit dinner alone with a woman at a nice restaurant, not because it's breaking a rule, but because it feels inhospitable. The space would be working against us, not for us.[13]

Grigg's advice has the marks of wisdom to it. Cultivating hospitality while pursuing holiness and generosity gives us specific reference points to establish healthy boundaries while still allowing us to extend friendship to men and women around us.

What's particularly beautiful is that this kind of friendship hospitality—by the family of God toward the family of God and the world—can be practiced by anyone, regardless of age or marital status. Jeremy and I *delight* in the rich friendships flourishing among the college-aged men and women we mentor as they increasingly use the language of family with each other and find creative ways to live into it. As each year with our students goes by, we feel increasingly like proud older siblings, cheering them on as they learn to love one another better as brothers and sisters. They're practicing what it means to create safe, welcoming spaces for one another, and they're welcoming their unbelieving friends into their "college family" circles for Jesus' sake too. It's magnificent to watch.

Yes, men and women can be friends. I see it in Jesus' example. I see it among those in the early church. I see it in our church now where there are real friendships between men and women that have the hallmarks of health and holiness, based as they are on kinship in Christ.

Yes, it sometimes does get awkward. And sometimes there are warning flags that a worrisome tension is developing in a friendship. In those situations, we need wisdom, which is where we turn in our next chapter.

CHAPTER 7

WHAT ABOUT ALL THE HORROR STORIES?

You mean you still talk to your ex-boyfriends?"

"I still talk to some of them," I said.

My friend was shocked. Incredulous, even. We were talking about an article we'd both read, and I mentioned that an ex-boyfriend had been the one to send it my way. Her eyes were popping. I could see the questions brimming under the surface: *Does your husband know? Is it appropriate? Is it awkward? Should I fire you as my mentor?*

Whether or not I'm still in touch with an old boyfriend varies with each relationship. There are some I don't stay in touch with because it's confusing or painful or just a little weird for one or both of us. I dated someone for several years before meeting my husband, and things were confused and confusing for some time after we broke up, so we didn't talk much then. But these days, it feels more like we're old friends, because we are. And we're still connected in Christ.

When I hear from someone I once dated, I consider several things before responding: who is reaching out, where he is in his life, the medium the message comes through (a comment on Facebook, an email, a call), the message itself (a funny cat meme, a lunch invitation), and what our past correspondence has been like (has he shown himself to be a friend to my marriage, or does he communicate as if my husband doesn't exist?). All these factors come into play. So, the answer to the question of whether or not I talk to an ex-boyfriend is "It depends."

PROVERBIAL WISDOM: IT DEPENDS

"Answer not a fool according to his folly, lest you be like him yourself," says Proverbs 26:4. And the very next verse is "Answer a fool according to his folly, lest he be wise in his own eyes" (v. 5). Conflicts such as these used to drive my inner rule-follower bonkers. Which is it, wise guy? Should I answer a fool or not? What's the right thing to do? *Just make up your mind, already.*

Wisdom's answers can be infuriatingly vague. *It depends* doesn't seem to be an answer at all, but a dodge, a duck, a cop-out. But in truth, there is much in our world that isn't a question of blatant right or wrong so much as a question of *discernment*. The nature of wisdom is contextual—it asks what is right or wrong depending on the situation and people involved. Sometimes it might be wise to answer a fool, and sometimes it's probably best to ignore a fool. For example, consider when one of my children declares, "I'm never going to school again." Sometimes I just let the statement go and keep steering that child toward the door. And other times I sit down and ask that child to imagine what would happen if he or she did, in fact, give up on school. Does he think he'd never have to do anything hard again? Does she think there would be no unwanted work at home—that life without school means unlimited free play? Think again, buster. Both ignoring and reasoning can be wise options. *It depends*.

We need wisdom not only because life is too complex for any one set of rules but also because only wisdom is flexible enough to adapt to new contexts. Rules aimed at maintaining the status quo aren't enough to keep us faithful. Our hearts bend toward loopholes, and each cultural shift places new pressure points on our souls. One of the mantras of the sixteenth-century Protestant Reformation was *semper reformanda*, which means "always reforming." Wesley Hill adroitly explained, "The skewing effects of original sin will ensure that the status quo will always be in need of reform."[1] It's true. Even with something as simple as a diet, I couldn't stick to a new eating plan for three days before I'd start calculating innovative ways I could cheat without technically "cheating."

This battle is a tale as old as time. In his letter to the church at Colossae, the apostle Paul challenged a group who, in their earnest desire to battle against sin, set up a whole bunch of rules and requirements to help the community remain faithful. Paul did not mince words: "Why . . . do you submit to regulations— 'Do not handle, Do not taste, Do not touch'?" We might add, "Do not text!" Paul goes on to point out that such rules "indeed have the appearance of wisdom . . . but they are of no value in stopping the indulgence of the flesh" (Colossians 2:20–23). And more to the point, not only do they *not* keep us from sin, as Philip Yancey succinctly puts it, "Legalism fails miserably at the one thing it is supposed to do: encourage obedience."[2]

PUTTING RULES IN (THEIR) PLACE

Strict rules are no guarantee we won't sin. God's first rules in the Garden of Eden were perfectly clear and easy to understand, but all it took was one beguiling snake to show that where there's a will, there's a way to flout the rule. That's not to say rules are pointless, though. They serve a vital purpose. Yet even the best rules can't deal with the root problem of sin (Romans 8:3). So what place do laws have? Just as we put a plaster cast around a broken bone to set it and allow it to heal in the right direction, so, too, God gave the law to his broken people to set us on the right path and guide us toward growth in righteousness. The law doesn't heal what's broken, but it provides structural support (and protection) for a wounded system.

The goal of the law was always freedom—to train and develop internal strength rather than constrain by external limits. The apostle Paul describes the law as a "tutor," given to instruct and teach children until they could move into the freedom that maturity brings (Galatians 4:1–4, 5:1 KJV). This image makes all the more sense to me as I try to parent my own children. My goal in creating rules about bedtimes, teeth brushing, and homework is not that my kids would obey my rules as ends in themselves, but for them to grow up to be adults who have internalized stewardship for their rhythms of rest, oral hygiene, and diligent work. True adulthood looks like the maturity to make the right choices, even when no one is watching.

Or, in the language of the classics, it looks like cultivating *virtue*: those character traits formed by a lifetime of making good choices. Character is *etched* into us, one small choice at a time. Each decision we make leaves its mark and shapes us in a particular direction. Practicing doing good (by obeying the law) forms ability and agility in our moral muscle, just as practicing multiplication tables improves math fluency or practicing scales increases our musical skills. Musical masters are called *virtuosos* for just this reason: their excellence results from practiced skill. As Karen Swallow Prior puts it, virtue "is a habit of moral character, which, because it is a habit, becomes second nature."[3]

In this sense maturity is correlated not necessarily with age, but with how much practice we've had and how deeply engrained those good habits become. And wisdom—being something the Scriptures say can be *sought* and *learned* and *acquired*[4]—speaks of the skillful, moral decision-making that accompanies a person of mature character.

The law—or whatever rules of conduct we're discussing—does play a role in helping us to learn and conform to the "shape" of holiness. I imagine the shaping of our characters and the formation of wisdom as something akin to potters molding lumps of clay into vessels that are both beautiful and useful. I imagine God giving the law as a potter's hands guide the formation of a pot, constraining the clay and defining its boundaries (Jeremiah 18:1–12). I imagine the work of the Holy Spirit to be like the potter's fingers pressed into the middle of the pot, shaping from the inside and working in tandem with the pressure from the outside to stretch the vessel into a finer, taller piece of art. I imagine the law—with its lessons on love applied to neighborliness and worship and justice—shaping us with its rules from the outside, while at the same time the Holy Spirit works on cultivating love, joy, peace, kindness, gentleness, faithfulness, and self-control from the inside. On the potter's wheel, the shaping is continuous. And sometimes dizzying.

To become a versatile and useful vessel, clay must allow itself to be shaped by conforming to the artist's hand. If the shaping force of the potter's hands is removed too quickly, the clay will become lopsided and wobble, the loss of stability threatening the entire piece. It's not hard to see the spiritual and moral corollary. When we separate ourselves from the shaping force of God's law and God's hands, life inevitably wobbles. There are painful consequences and sometimes tragic outcomes, and it would not be fair to write a book about vision for healthy, mature, beautiful relationships between men and women without acknowledging that sometimes things go terribly, awfully wrong.

WHEN BAD THINGS HAPPEN: INFIDELITY, ABUSE, AND SEXUAL UNFAITHFULNESS

I wish I didn't know half the things I now know about the evil that happens behind closed doors. In classrooms, bedrooms, and churches everywhere and in devastating numbers, people do the most awful things. Marriage covenants are betrayed. Children are groomed, groped, and raped. Quiet clicks on websites bring violent and vile sexual imagery into darkened rooms. People abuse and hurt each other in horrifying ways. When I read the news of the latest scandal perpetuated by a politician, a pastor, or a parent, I sometimes wonder if God feels the same way he did in the days of Noah, regretting he ever made humankind (Genesis 6:5–6).

My own childhood was marked by marital infidelity, and in adulthood I've spent some of my most painful hours in grief and rage at sexual sin: loved ones betrayed, loved ones sexually violated. My belief that men and women can and should be in healthy relationships is not borne of a Pollyanna-esque naïveté that glosses over the depths of human depravity. On more than one occasion, I have played the "if only" game, wondering if only something had been different, if only there had been some other constraint, some other factor, some other check, whether a certain tragedy wouldn't have happened. But the hard truth is, people inclined to do evil will do evil. And if there's a rule as an obstacle, they'll find a way to hurdle it. We all do. In writing his extensive list of sins people dabble in, there is a reason the apostle Paul included a catch-all category for humans who "invent ways of doing evil" (Romans 1:30 NIV).

Sexual infidelity and abuse ultimately result from a lack of character, not a lack of constraints. The "safest" dog isn't the one on the shortest leash; it's the one with the best training. It's the one that responds when called, doesn't dash after whatever flits across its path, knows the rhythms and rules of the household, and lives peaceably within them. So, too, with "safe people."

Rules might shorten our leashes, but self-restraint and good character are the real protectors. Wisdom calls us to mature in goodness and

> **SEXUAL INFIDELITY AND ABUSE ULTIMATELY RESULT FROM A LACK OF CHARACTER, NOT A LACK OF CONSTRAINTS.**

godliness, continually developing our ability to "distinguish good from evil" (Hebrews 5:14). But wisdom also has a healthy awareness of our immense capacity for sin and self-deception—in both ourselves and in others. As the old hymn confesses, "prone to wander, Lord I feel it." We know the good we should do, yet we so often do just the opposite, as Paul lamented in Romans 7. This is why a regular practice of self-examination and confession are so important in our spiritual formation; even though we trust that we are in the process of being "conformed to the image of his Son" (Romans 8:29), we are also sober about the fact that we're not there yet.

Wisdom can guard and guide us in situations for which there are no specific rules, and this applies all the more in the realm of sexual ethics. Jesus warned his disciples that if they even *looked* at a woman lustfully, they had already crossed a line (Matthew 5:27–30). Everybody knew the rule against adultery—that was black and white. And in first-century Judaism, women and men were pretty covered up clothing-wise, and kept fairly separate quarters socially. Yet conservative social customs about modesty and rabbinical rules about avoiding the opposite sex weren't enough to keep sin at bay. Sexual unfaithfulness, Jesus taught, needs to be nipped in the bud right between looking and looking *lustfully*. In other words, you could technically be on the right side of the rules and still be in sexually dangerous territory. Jesus called his disciples to radical transparency and self-scrutiny, cutting across legalisms and requiring them to adopt what Bible scholar Alice Mathews described as "a radical change of heart that would make it unnatural for a man to want to exploit or degrade a woman."[5]

I experienced a taste of what Jesus was warning against early in my marriage. Engagement is notoriously a time for sexual temptation and testing, so perhaps I wasn't expecting to find myself battling testing once I was actually married. Wasn't I supposed to be in the safety zone now? I was happily married and deeply attracted to my husband, and so I felt doubly shocked to find myself strangely attracted to somebody else too. A friend. A married friend. There hadn't been any flirting, or anything untoward said or done by me or him (I don't think he ever knew), but *I knew* I was noticing him more than I should. I would dwell over certain conversations we'd had. I would mentally linger. And even while I was confident it wouldn't go anywhere, I knew something wasn't right, and I couldn't just go along with "being his friend" without somehow acknowledging the tension I felt.

One afternoon I sat on a bench under the dappled shade of an oak tree and confessed my jumble of thoughts to an older, married friend. I think I expected her to be shocked, disapproving. But she nodded and listened, then answered quite simply, "Well, that's probably not the last time you'll feel an attraction to someone you're not married to. We're sexual beings, and if we are aware of some kind of spark, it's good to pay attention to it and make sure it doesn't become a flame."

Attraction is normal. Sexual dynamics are part of how we're made. But what I did with those dynamics is what mattered. Confession was a good start. And then practicing a little distance—redirecting myself both physically and mentally as needed—were the things I needed to do.

A TIME FOR FRIENDSHIP, A TIME FOR FENCES

If discernment and wisdom are at the heart of developing healthy relationships between men and women, then it's important at this point to make some distinctions—to discern, if you will—about who precisely these guidelines we've been exploring are for.

The short answer is they are primarily for Christian women and men in the church. While the principles could also be helpful to people in vocational ministry, that's not my primary focus. The reason for this is simple: the rules are different for those in ministry, just as they are for anyone in a position of authority or leadership, such as counselors, teachers, children's workers, or youth workers. Such relationships are not "between friends" in the same way as we've been discussing in previous chapters. Sibling and friendship relationships are primarily horizontal: they're conversations among peers and equals, or at least conversations in a fairly neutral, communally accessible space (around a dinner table, for example).

However, in situations where there's an authority, maturity, or vulnerability gap between two people, the onus is on the person with more authority or power to set and maintain appropriate boundaries. There are good reasons why adults avoid saying explicit or confusing things around kids: as the older and hopefully wiser generation, we bear the responsibility for curtailing our conversations to what's appropriate and helpful for little ears. We don't want to expose kids to things they don't yet have the maturity to process. And there are good reasons why counselors need training to serve people who have suffered trauma. Traumatic experiences deeply affect a person's ability to trust and establish intimacy, and a wise counselor needs to do intentional trauma-informed work to create a safe space for those conversations.

It is the responsibility of the adult, the counselor, or the leader—not the child, the trauma survivor, or the subordinate—to safeguard what is appropriate, sexually and otherwise, in any relationship. One of the hallmarks of unhealthy character in an adult is creating a manipulative relationship with a person who is vulnerable or under their authority and acting as if the relationship were a friendship marked by mutuality (such as a youth pastor "dating" one of his teens or a therapist sharing their own marital struggles with a client). For example, they might recast abuse as an "affair." Author and pastor Ed Stetzer pulled no punches when he noted, "Children, including teenagers, don't commit adultery with adults. There is no 'consent.' Our courts have rightly determined that teens are incapable of consenting to sex with an adult. . . . This isn't infidelity. It's not an 'affair.' This is abuse."[6]

What calls for greater caution in these relationships is the significant *power differentials*. In the privacy of a counselor's or pastor's office, I might disclose very different and much deeper things than I would to a friend, even if that same counselor or pastor could well be a friend in a different context. My disclosure level—and thus my vulnerability and exposure—is much greater in those circumstances. And that's a significant factor that distinguishes such relationships from more general friendships.

Another factor is that this sharing and vulnerability is not reciprocal. A pastor, counselor, or adult in authority might be entrusted with very deep and personal things by someone, but it is not appropriate for them to share details about their own spiritual darkness, sexual struggles, or personal convictions in return. It's not a two-way friendship. The purpose of the relationship is different, and thus the protections for that relationship need to be different.

Whenever there is a power differential, the issue is not so

much that men and women can't or shouldn't be friends, but that there are power and responsibility dynamics at play. A relationship between a person in a position of authority or leadership and anyone who falls under their authority or leadership is something other than friendship. This is why it is often so difficult for people in ministry to navigate friendships, because it's not always clear whether a person is inviting you closer because of the spiritually significant role you play in their lives, or because they are offering friendship. Pastors and their spouses often carry very deep loneliness: they long for friendly peer relationships within their Christian family, but the responsibilities and burdens of their roles don't allow for reciprocity. Healthy self-care for counselors, ministers, and leaders in shepherding roles requires that they meet their needs for community legitimately, and not illegitimately with those under their authority or care.

Such power differentials and complications are the reason my friend Talia, a marriage and family therapist, chooses not to participate in small-group Bible studies or prayer circles that include a client. It's just too hard, for her and the client, to share both a spiritual-sibling/friendship space as well as client/therapist space. It's why when I speak at conferences, I don't accept invitations to join the small group discussions after plenary sessions. Who wants to share openly when the speaker is at your table? Not me.

Remember the small group of friends I mentioned in the previous chapter? I think one of the reasons we've found one another is because we all have significant leadership roles in our professional lives. At one point the group included a youth pastor, a college professor, a national ministry trainer, a Bible teacher, and a therapist. In our jobs we have people we enjoy and care for deeply, but it's often just too complicated to try forging friend-ships in our vocational spaces given the dynamics of our roles. And so we have each other in our group, where there are no power differentials and the relationships are mutual.

Relationships in which there is a power differential are by definition not mutual; they are not peer relationships. Nonmutual relationships are inherently riskier because one party is always more vulnerable or exposed than the other. And, again, it is always the responsibility of the person with more power or authority to safeguard the boundaries. It's not the child's job to call out an adult's off-color joke, nor a client's responsibil-ity to point out that their therapist shouldn't have shared what they did. It's not uncommon for people to develop emotional attachments or sexual attraction to mentors, pastors, leaders, or anyone to whom they've disclosed deep and vulnerable things. But just as doctors need professional boundaries when dealing with their naked and vulnerable patients, anyone in a position of authority needs to maintain appropriate boundaries with those in their care—especially when that care makes them privy to the nakedness of people's souls. Emotional sharing is a real form of intimacy, and it needs real, appropriate boundaries. When a leader exploits the intimacy of a professional context for personal satisfaction, it is not a reciprocal love relationship. It is an abuse of power.

Back in the early nineties, I remember reading of the Clinton-Lewinsky scandal with both horror and confusion. I'm about the same age as Monica Lewinsky, and I was a law student at the time the scandal broke. It was easy to imagine what it might have been like to be an intern in such a high-powered place, and how blindingly disorienting the attention and praise of a person in such an influential position might be. Even after more than twenty years, Lewinsky still has difficulty parsing her feelings and the nature of their relationship, writing that what she first experienced as depression was really a deep grief: "Grief for having been betrayed first by someone I thought was my friend, and then by a man I thought had cared for me."[7]

From her perspective the relationship looked like friendship, or maybe affection. But then again, just how free was she to say no or yes to their relationship? Who could say no to the power and charisma of the most powerful man in the world? Whether the president shared her feelings of attachment is irrelevant. The Oval Office carries power, and it was the president's power to steward. Or, in this case, to abuse.

Christians are as vulnerable to these dangers as anyone else. Recent years have brought wave after wave of disclosures about pastors and priests who made inappropriate and unwanted advances on staff members and parishioners. Speaking of her own experience of such unhealthy dynamics, Nancy Beach, who was the first female teaching pastor of a large Chicago church, said, "We wonder and despair: Can men and women work together without falling to sexual sin?" But she also acknowledged the complex power dynamics that played a significant role in what happened, something journalist Morgan Lee summarizes as "an inner circle of leaders that were complicit in enabling the primary leader's bad behavior because members of the group directly benefited from this leader's power."[8]

Beach admits that while she didn't know of the sexual sin at first, she did see abuses of power, and it is the privileges of privacy and trust conferred by power that often create a cloak of secrecy for evil. "Among the many dark gifts of power is distance," writes Andy Crouch, "distance from accountability, distance from consequences, distance from the pain we cause others, distance from self-knowledge, distance from friendship, distance from the truth."[9] Whether it's the Oval Office, the conference room, private bathrooms adjoining executive suites, or King David's palace rooftop, one of the "perks" of leadership is that it can shield us from accountability.

It was an acute awareness of the temptations of power that informed Billy Graham's decision early in his ministry to make himself rigorously accountable to others. The "Billy Graham Rule," as it's now known, describes his commitment to never be alone with a woman other than his wife. But Graham's resolution was part of a much broader pledge. Early in his ministry Graham and some fellow evangelists had listed some of the biggest pitfalls and temptations they'd seen derail ministries, and they made solemn resolutions to safeguard themselves accordingly. Knowing that money, pride, and fame were temptations, they made commitments to financial scrutiny, partnership with local churches, and tempered publicity. And knowing that sex scandals had wrecked many kingdom ventures, they committed to radical public accountability in their dealings with women. Billy Graham's rule, for all the rap that it has taken about keeping men and women separate, was at its heart about the faithful stewardship of the power that comes with ministry responsibility.[10]

Other evangelical pastors, leaders, and even a vice president of the United States have adopted similar positions, seeking to "avoid impropriety" at all costs.[11] And, given the power dynamics and vulnerabilities that come with such jobs, thinking about how one stewards one's role well is vital. But for the rest of us, the danger exists that we might conflate good practices for everyone with the "higher fences," such as the Billy Graham Rule, designed for the unique responsibilities of leaders. When we overapply boundaries that rightly belong in one context to *every* context, we do so at the expense of allowing friendships and work partnerships to flourish.

Nancy Beach summarized it well:

> Our fear of potential moral failure may well drive us to conclude that the answer is to go back to our safe comfort zones, to separate the genders as much as possible, to not invite women to the leadership table, and also to establish twenty more rules—we can't be in the same elevator or anywhere near one another so that no one will have the opportunity to sin. . . . I believe any overcorrection along those lines would be a huge mistake, a tragic loss for our communities of faith.[12]

We need to respond with wisdom, not react with fear. In the wake of high-profile sexual scandals among Christian leaders, my home church made a decision to replace all the solid wood doors in the office with glass-paned ones. I respected that. Our church leadership wanted to proactively create systems which take into account the temptations that come with power. Having glass doors allows pastoral conversations to be visible and yet still private. It was a move toward literal transparency. And I know that the pastors at my church have their own personal commitments and accountability structures, including people they check in with regularly to ask them hard questions.

These boundaries—both the actual doors and the social framework of accountability—are part of what give me confidence that I can call my pastors *leaders*, *brothers*, and also *friends*. It is sometimes tricky navigating which conversation is shared in which context, but with awareness of the relational dynamics at play and humility and wisdom as our guides, it is possible. There are times when I might share something personal with a pastor, who also happens to be a friend. But when we and our spouses get together for game night, that conversation I had with the pastor is off the table, even though our spouses may both have heard about it. We walk this line with caution: some things are ministry/pastoral-care talk, some are shared in marital confidence, and other things are up for conversation among friends. We don't always get it right. We need wisdom and we need to be honest with ourselves and one another. We need to cultivate *prudence*, that antiquated word that basically means caution and foresight. "Prudence is wisdom in practice," writes Karen Swallow Prior.[13] It anticipates the possible dangers and plans its route accordingly.

But most of our relationships within the church community are a lot less complex, and don't bear nearly as much risk or vulnerability. Consequently, we have more freedom there. But as always, true freedom needs to be guided and governed by character. It is our internal moral compass that makes us safe—or not safe—people to be around. And of course Jesus was the perfect example of this.

THE MAN WITH NO RULES AND PERFECT BOUNDARIES

It seems Jesus was always getting into trouble for flouting "the rules," or at least the conventional wisdom of his day. He healed people on the Sabbath. He wasn't a stickler for ceremonial washing. He ate with tax collectors and sinners. But this is not to say he had no concern for righteousness. Jesus paid taxes (Matthew 17:24–27). He submitted to authorities as appropriate (John 18:36). He always told the truth. He had no "leash" to constrain him, but he had perfect self-control. He also had perfect wisdom (Colossians 2:2–3), embodied and expressed in real, intimate, appropriate relationships.

He could sit and talk privately with a woman with a well-known, sexually checkered past (John 4:7–30), or let another such woman massage and kiss his feet in public (Luke 7:36–39)—without the encounters becoming dangerous. They were undeniably intimate interactions, but what made them safe was Jesus himself. He was the ultimate "safe person," always clear on his own motives and true to his own character.

Andy Crouch observes that Jesus "offered no false intimacy— his biographer John said that he entrusted himself to no one, because he knew what was in every person's heart (John 2:24– 25)—but he kept no distance either. He let the children come to him (Matthew 19:14). He let Mary sit at his feet and let another Mary wash his feet with her tears (Luke 7:36–50; 10:39)."[14]

After his resurrection, when Mary at last recognized him at the garden tomb, Jesus gave a different instruction. "Do not cling to me," he said (John 20:17). Touching his feet may have been appropriate before, but Jesus let her know there had now been a shift in their relationship. Jesus' transition from a regular body to his resurrected body evidently required changes in how people related to him. He still had a physical body (John 20:24–27), and he was still able to enjoy a good fish fry (John 21:12–14), but he apparently no longer needed to use doors to get in and out of a room (John 20:19).

For Mary, it meant she and Jesus would no longer be traveling companions, and she shouldn't touch his feet. Rather, now was the time for her to go and bear witness to Jesus being her resurrected Lord. This was wisdom in action: Jesus establishing boundaries and framing the relationships around him appropriately for a new context.

Recognizing shifts in a relationship calls for wisdom. It calls for self-awareness and more than a little self-regulation. Sometimes relationships between friends change, and the guidelines that once applied don't quite fit any more. And on that note we turn to the topic of dating, and how we might navigate a shift from siblings in Christ, to friends, to something more.

CHAPTER 8

WILL YOU DRIVE WITH ME?

I could tell dozens of stories about missed connections, frustrated intentions, and awkward declarations between Christian men and women. Hundreds, even. Some delightful, some devastating, some totally cringe-worthy.

I never expected to be the custodian of so many tales of dating drama, but it goes with the territory for someone like me who's spent years in young adult ministry. I hear stories of people being friend-zoned, of unrequited crushes, of bad first dates and dead-end conversations. I get asked questions about whether it's okay to date at all, and if so, how? There are questions about how to cope with sexual desire if one is not dating, and even more so if one is. There are questions about how to know if it's time to start dating, or—and this is even harder—whether it's time to break up. And, in the midst of hearing all the awkward stories, I have often found myself telling more than a few awkward stories of my own.

MISSED CONNECTIONS

I cleared my throat and took a deep breath before I dialed. He answered on the second ring. "Hi, I got the flowers," I said. "I was calling to say thank you."

"You're welcome," he replied.

Awkward. Silence.

"So . . . I just called to say thanks for the flowers. They're lovely," I repeated.

"I'm glad," he said. "It was my pleasure."

More. Awkward. Silence. And then we hung up.

The above is an accurate transcript of a phone call in the first few weeks of meeting the man I would later marry. The short version of the story is that he'd moved to a new city, and a friend of a friend had reached out to help him find housing. The friend of that friend was me. I knew of some leads and passed those on. I also knew Jeremy was enrolling in a program at the seminary from which I'd just graduated, and I invited a couple of people who would be in his incoming class to come over for a barbeque that weekend. Knowing they'd soon be his seminary family, I invited him to join us for dinner, which is how we met.

Somewhere along the line, though, it was apparently

unclear to him whether I was being a community-builder or a relationship-bidder, so he sent me flowers in an effort to clarify any mixed signals. He was clearly interested in more. I was not. But my mother raised me to always say thank you for gifts, so I called to do just that. He accepted my thanks and noted the painful lack of reciprocity. End of phone call. Super awkward. We didn't talk again for weeks.

Yes, we could be friends. We could be siblings in Christ. But I didn't want to date. Obvious spoiler alert: things changed. I'm a little less awkward when he gives me flowers these days. So that's one dating story I sometimes share.

Another story from dating yesteryear was that weird in-between space in my friendship with Karabo, a classmate and friend in my first year of seminary. Our fellow students hailed from all over South Africa (and far beyond), and conversations about racial reconciliation and cultural difference were tender. We'd all come from such vastly different backgrounds. As we struggled through Greek and church history assignments together, we'd started to carve our way into living as the brothers and sisters we really were. It was hard, holy, good work.

By our second year, Karabo and I were serving on the student leadership body and spending a significant amount of time working together. One day, as we walked back to class, he took my hand. I'd never detected any vibe of interest from him, so I looked over with some surprise. His face was as it had been before, animated in conversation. No sneaky smile. No flirtation. I didn't know what to make of it.

When he took my hand again a couple of days later, I was confused. In the smattering of relationships I'd had before, there had been a slow progression of meaningful looks and hints that preceded a casual brush of the hands, which then progressed to linking of fingers, which finally made its way to full-on hand-holding, which was a relationship-status changer in and of itself. This felt different, and I didn't understand it. Maybe dating was different in his culture?

So I asked. I braved the awkward and put the question to him: "So . . . you're holding my hand and I'm not sure what this means. I've only ever held hands with guys I'm dating, but this doesn't feel quite like that." He smiled and assured me that, really, it didn't mean anything more than that we were friends and we were walking together.

"Oh," I said, and then stammered to explain. "That's not what handholding meant as I was growing up." This was news to him, and we decided for the sake of it not being confusing—to me or anyone else—we'd be friends of the not-handholding type.

"While we're on the topic," he said, "can I mention something else?"

I nodded. This conversation was already different from any I'd had before—what else might be coming?

"Sometimes you touch my head," he said, pointing to his beautiful shaved dome. "That's intimate to me. Not something just a friend would do. So maybe also something to think about."

"Oh," I said again, this time a little embarrassed. I'd had no idea. But I was glad we'd talked. Both of us had made physical gestures of friendship that, to the other, had been interpreted as a bid for something more. Both of us had been confused. And it was a bit awkward to talk about it. But we did, and the honest communication helped us get beyond the awkwardness and into the realm of friends-who-are-siblings.

By contrast, things were less clear for my friend Eli. Eli had returned to our campus for a couple of years running with teams from his church on two-week evangelism and apologetics missions. Eli is ridiculously smart, funny, and self-effacing. He also has a Wikipedia-like memory and an incredible combination of razor-sharp wit and gentle demeanor. Eli was also unmarried, twenty years older than most members of the team, and wore the mantle of being the big brother of the group with grace. He spoke that way, too, addressing emails to "my little sister," and signing them from "your big brother." I was never confused by the nature of our friendship. It was close—so close—but not awkward.

When my life was split in two by tragedy halfway through my college years, it was Eli I emailed, and Eli who wrote compassionate, comforting words that had me muffling sobs in the law library computer room. In response to my email, he'd sent me two verses from the beginning of Job: "When Job's three friends heard of all this evil that had come upon him, they came. . . . to show him sympathy and comfort him. . . . They sat with him on the ground seven days and seven nights, and no one spoke a word to him, for they saw that his suffering was very great" (Job 2:11, 13). Then, as always, Eli treated me with the tender compassion of a big brother, as he did all the women in our campus fellowship.

So I was shocked when, a few months later, Eli mentioned that a mutual friend of ours—several years younger than me—had written him a "Dear John" letter, explaining that she didn't feel that way about him and gently rejecting an offer he was sure he hadn't made. She'd been "little sister" and he'd been "big brother" to her, just as he had to me, but for various reasons, she had read the situation differently. She didn't seem sure how to process a man so much older than her showing such interest and warmth. She wanted to be gentle yet clear about where they stood. Eli was a little surprised: Had he sent mixed signals? Did she think he'd been making advances rather than offering friendship? Things can get murky even with the best of intentions.

Navigating the space between kinship in Christ, friendship, and romantic interest is tricky and can be plagued by missed connections. There's no one right way to do it. I tell these stories to acknowledge it baldly: Yes, it's awkward. At times, painfully so.

I believe with all my heart that God has given us a *familial* framework for close, healthy, gendered relationships with the men and women around us, and that this matrix gives us a wise and safe space to start conversations about the nature of our relationships. I believe Jesus' forward-thinking and broad-ranging view of family protects us from a myopic view of intimacy that deems the nuclear family the be-all and end-all, often to the exclusion of developing broader, hospitable relationships within the church. Church should not be made up of the married, who are unavailable for relationships, and the unmarried, who are in a kind of relational holding pen. And church should not be segregated by sex, with women hanging only with women, and men hanging only with men. Rather, we should embody the New Testament model of church as a big family gathering, brothers and sisters around the table *together.*

Even so, the family framework does raise the question of dating, and how in the world one can move from a gendered brother/sister nonsexual relationship to one with "someone special," where a bit of sexy spark is totally part of the deal.

More than one young adult has asked me, "Wouldn't it just be easier to have arranged marriages?" I've sometimes joked that I could guarantee a *New York Times* bestseller by publishing a version of the Bible with an appendix titled, "Who You're Supposed to Marry." It would have saved so much time to look under "B" for "Bronwyn" and find Jeremy's name cross-referenced. But in the absence of a divinely inspired spouse appendix or a community of elders willing to matchmake on our behalf, chances are we are going to find our marriage partners ourselves, and that means we are going to have to date.

Dating is our cultural norm, the customary vehicle for how we get from one kind of relationship to another. Dating itself is a morally neutral thing, neither "good" nor "bad." In that sense, it's a bit like driving—it's the way we get from point A to point B given where and when we live in history. The Bible has no specific verses on how we date or drive, but we have general principles of character, neighborliness, and wisdom to rely on. Just as we can drive well or drive badly, we can date well or date badly. Scripture doesn't have anything to say about *whether* we should drive or date, but it has much to say about being considerate, neighborly, wise people in *how* we do these things. Dating well, then, might be described as an honest and healthy exploration of whether a relationship with a brother or sister in Christ might become *more*.

DATING IS THE ROAD TEST FOR THE ROAD TRIP

It goes without saying that our expectations and hopes for marriage are directly correlated to how we approach dating. We've already talked about a vision of marriage as an *intimate partnership*, side-by-side in service of God and the world. If that vision of marriage is beautiful and compelling to us, it means in dating we're looking for more than someone with whom we experience chemistry; we're looking for someone with whom we also experience camaraderie. That means the dating process is as much about evaluating *partnership* potential as it is about evaluating *passion* potential. With so much emphasis on evaluating passion in dating (the importance of it, how to handle it), we could do with a little refresher on evaluating partnership while dating.

> THE DATING PROCESS IS AS MUCH ABOUT EVALUATING *PARTNERSHIP* POTENTIAL AS IT IS ABOUT EVALUATING *PASSION* POTENTIAL.

One analogy I find helpful in this regard is that of marriage as a lifelong cross-country road trip. Our expectations of road trips are often shaped by other people's travel photos—sunrise pictures at the Grand Canyon, road signs at the entrance to Las Vegas, sunsets on Maui. We think of the Instagrammable moments when we drive down the world's most crooked street, summit a mountain, or see cute couples kissing at concerts in Nashville. We imagine taking and being in such photos ourselves one day. Road trips make great photo albums.

However, what makes a road trip really awesome or really awful is not the snapshot moments when both of you are smiling, but how you got along for the thousands of miles and hundreds of hours when it was just the two of you in the car with that endless ribbon of road unrolling toward the horizon. What happened when you got lost? Could you tolerate the other person's driving style? Did you feel safe with him or her at the wheel? Did you fight about music or agree on a playlist? Was one of you a stop-for-a-Big-Mac-every-two-hundred-miles person, while the other person frugally packed a cooler with sandwiches and granola bars? Could you find fun things to talk about and yet also travel in companionable silence? Did you laugh? A road trip might have the most incredible attractions with magnificent views, but if you bickered and fought all the way, it won't have been a good journey. And, on the other hand, maybe there are people with whom you'd drive five thousand miles to Boringtown in a car with no air conditioning just because you always enjoy one another's company.

Dating is the relational road test before you sign up for the lifelong cross-country road trip that is marriage. It helps to shift one's focus from life's Instagrammable moments (*Who would I like to be in a picture with at Mount Rushmore?*), to the trip itself (*Who would I be willing to drive with all the way to freaking Mount Rushmore?*). In a way, it really doesn't matter how much attraction and chemistry you had with Ms. or Mr. Gorgeous at the beginning of the trip. Thousands of miles of driving can be as much of a passion killer as a passion kindler, depending on how the relational road test went.

CARPOOL KARAOKE

In dating, you begin by taking a number of shorter, about-town car rides with someone to figure out how you might do together on a longer trip sometime in the future. There will be a first time when one of you says, "Would you like to drive together?" and that first trip is usually somewhere nearby, and possibly with others in the car. This is where a church-as-family mind-set can help in the dating process.

Perhaps that first short drive might be with someone you've already been in the car with a bunch of times because—as members of the same church community—it's customary to carpool with friends. But at some point, dating would mean the difference between someone saying, "Anyone want to carpool?" and making a plan to pick up one specific person. In time, the community expects the two of you to be together often in the comings and goings of life. Sometimes others will ride with you. Sometimes it will be just the two of you. Sometimes you take turns driving. Some trips are short. Others longer. Sometimes you're running errands. Sometimes you're on your way to church. Over time, you'll see this driving buddy in a bunch of different contexts, and in conversation with different people. You'll have taken short drives with their parent(s) and best friends, and seen how they treat the homeless guy on the corner when you exit the parking lot. You'll get an idea of when they're friendly, when they're tense. How they respond when someone cuts them off in traffic, or when they miss the turn off and get lost. And on all of these road test trips, you're gathering information about how you might do as travel partners on a longer journey.[1]

Maybe one day you'll have done enough about-town errands to feel confident planning longer trips together. At this point you know which map app you agree on for the journey, you've successfully packed the trunk a couple of times like a two-player Tetris game, and you can plan out a route that hits a couple of things that are on each—or both—of your bucket lists. The prospect of a long-haul trip now seems less like a wild whim of an idea everyone should do at some point and more like something you specifically want to do—and want to do *together*. And maybe that would be a great time to consider putting a ring on all those plans to seal the deal—Trip Advisor meets Match.com.

It's a labored analogy, perhaps, but the advantage of the analogy is twofold. First, the road-trip metaphor sets a more realistic long-term expectation about what marriage feels like. Second, it can help to think of dating as a collection of lower-risk, short-term opportunities to find out what someone might be like as a long-term road-trip buddy. The fact that some around-town car trips happen with a mixed assortment of friends and in a variety of situations also helps us think about dating with some more freedom. Dating could be something we do as part of our regular rhythms in community life.

Even so, there are still challenges to overcome. One concern I hear from young men in the church is that it often feels so high risk to date. I recall one nervous student confessing he had a crazy crush on a lovely young woman in our church, and asking my husband and me for advice on how to ask her out. "What kinds of things have you two talked about before?" my husband asked, and the young man stared sheepishly at the floor. He'd never actually talked to the girl. Just admired her from afar. Despite being a sociable guy with friends throughout the group, he'd never known how to start a conversation with someone he *liked*. What was the first step? Wasn't there an app for that?

Our advice was to try getting to know her first—there were definitely ways he could do this without having to commit to full-fledged dating from the get-go. And once they'd "carpooled in community" a couple of times, maybe he'd find that inviting her to coffee would come a little easier. Our point was this: if we're not living in a community where men and women can talk to one another as brothers and sisters, starting that first conversation might feel like crossing a giant abyss. But if we're in a community where we work together, talk together, "carpool" together, and worship together as friendly brothers and sisters, then the segue to having longer, more sustained conversations in dating isn't as vast a leap.

I often come across young adults who tell me with some anxiety that they're not sure they know how to date. I'm eager to encourage them that, really, they already know more than they think. Dating (and marriage) are not some *other* category of relationship that requires a completely *other* set of mysterious skills. The skills they already have in building friendships are the same skills to bring to bear in dating. If they know how to have a conversation, take turns at washing dishes or riding shotgun, laugh around a dinner table, and talk through a conflict, those are the *exact* same skills that make dating (and marriage) possible and pleasurable. Dating is just a particular application of a relational skill set they've already been working on all their lives. The skills we develop as friends and coworkers and roommates are 100 percent the skills we bring into dating and marriage. If I have observed someone being a generous listener, quick to forgive, a considerate roommate, and servant-hearted team-player, then I feel pretty confident that they *do* know how to date—even if they've never actually been on a date.

Done well, our collected carpool experiences (some of which may include actual Carpool Karaoke, which my silly, song-loving self would consider a sign of a 98 percent compatibility) can give us a great idea of whether we might be able to go the distance with someone. Knowing we have permission to become familiar with one another as brothers and sisters can do a whole lot to make those initial conversations a little more natural and fun.

"HOW FAR CAN WE GO?"

Of all the questions I am asked about dating relationships, two come up most often. The first is "How can I know if this person is 'the one'?" In response to this question, I usually give some version of the "Can you go on a road trip with them and not want to commit murder?" spiel.

The second question is "How far can we go?" In other words, when, why, and how fast can (or should) a dating couple entertain some of that *eros* dynamic? Here again, remembering that we are part of the family of God points us toward wisdom. The brother-sister relationship is a gendered but not sexualized one, but a dating relationship is different in that it absolutely adds some relational hot sauce to the mix. What's appropriate? And how can we handle that well?

At the big-picture level, part of the answer to this is to do the work of peeling back the expectations and assumptions that lie beneath the question (as the first chapters of this book aim to do). Our answer to the "How far can we go?" question will be of little help (and have little traction) if a dating couple believes deep down that sex really is the truest and best indicator of (1) whether they love each other, and (2) whether they're compatible. It doesn't matter whether our discipleship advice is "stick to handholding," "no more than kissing," or "anything but all the way," if the story they've heard about sex is that it is the best, only, and truest way to know whether this is love, and whether that spark will last. "True love waits" advice is just not going to cut it in these conditions. With enough voices shouting, "It's your body, your choice, and a private decision with no other consequences," and "as long as there's consent, it's okay," pledges and purity rings have a short shelf life.

If our teens, students, and singles in the church are swimming in cultural waters that recognize and affirm our sexuality only when it is genitally expressed, then any counsel about limiting sexual contact will sound to those ears like Christians are peddling relationships with no *real* possibility of intimacy and fulfillment. That's part of why we need to address the underlying stories we tell ourselves about belonging, our bodies, sexuality, and intimacy.

So for sure, part of our sexual discipleship and dating advice needs to take on the bigger picture that you can be *fully* male and *fully* female, and you *can* be in intimate, close relationships with people—even if *no one* is holding your hand or wanting to remove your underwear. I am absolutely convinced that speaking often and admiringly about men and women living beautiful, compelling lives within a network of healthy relationships can and does take some of the edge off the felt need for dating relationships to push sexual boundaries. However, I am also well aware that when a young woman sits on my couch and asks, "So, how far can I go?" to give an answer such as "Well, you know you're fully female and fully loved even without this guy, right?" is infuriatingly vague.

So in short, my advice to those considering how much to show or how much to share while dating is to ask themselves two questions.

1. WHAT HABITS OR EXPECTATIONS ARE WE FORMING WITH THIS BEHAVIOR?

Are we being disproportionately emotionally intimate in sharing too much, too soon? Are we creating expectations that dates always end with physical contact—and a truckload of unfulfilled longings? Are we creating habits of avoiding awkward conversations or boredom by defaulting to physical closeness? Are we making choices that fuel our imagination and appetites in helpful or harmful ways? This one applies to things the couple does together as well as personal habits, such as porn.

Much of the gray area I get asked about (including questions about naked selfies, masturbation, and oral sex) becomes much less gray when a couple considers what habits and expectations their sexual behavior is building in them. How is this choice teaching me to want or expect something? If we see our sexual behaviors as, in some way, shaping our sexual character and future, then the question is not just "Is this particular activity okay?" but actually "How is this particular activity changing me and this relationship? And do I respect and want to go in the direction it's taking me?" [2] As brothers and sisters in Christ, we play a role in one another's spiritual formation, so it matters how our dating habits are forming not only us but also the brother or sister we're dating.

2. HOW WILL I FEEL ABOUT OUR INTIMACY CHOICES IF WE BREAK UP?

No couple likes to entertain the thought that a breakup might happen, but thinking about how they might still stay in the same community of believers after a breakup can be a helpful way to navigate physical and emotional intimacy. If we've shared deeply intimate things, or if we've seen one another's souls or bodies naked—then it makes going back to worshiping alongside one another as just brother and sister very tough. Going too far too fast does more than just compromise the couple; it can make things really awkward for the community around them if things go south. [3] Stewarding our sexuality in dating in a way that we could still stay in the same church (and be friends with the next person they date without feeling shame!) would be something to celebrate. Realizing we're part of a broader community—whether or not we're dating—can help us choose behaviors that protect our bodies and together affirm God's intent for sexuality.[4]

NAVIGATING A BETTER BREAKUP

As hard as it sometimes is for Christian couples to *start* dating, it can be even harder for them to figure out how and when to *stop* dating. A breakup makes a wide ripple in a community, and couples often wonder whether it's advisable—or even permissible—to break up. Shouldn't they just try harder? Be nicer? Forgive? Do the concerns and misgivings they have mean there's something really wrong and they should act on it? If they choose to stay in the relationship, does that mean they're *settling*? If they go, does that mean they're being *unrealistically picky*?

So let me say a few words about breaking up. First, it's okay for dating couples to break up. That's part of what the dating process is about: figuring out whether you want to commit to the long term. Saying "No, I don't think this is going and growing in a healthy direction for the long term" is a *successful* answer to the dating question because at least now you know. You've learned something about yourself and about the other person.

It might be hard to give breakups such a positive spin, but consider this analogy. When Jeremy and I first started looking to buy a home, we thought we had a fairly good idea of what we wanted in a house. But then we started actually visiting houses, and I discovered a host of opinions I didn't know I had.

I discovered I have strong preferences about how far the kitchen is from the living room. I discovered I care about whether there's carpet all the way to the front door. I discovered I have an irrationally emotional dislike of popcorn ceilings. I toured dozens of houses I would never, ever want to buy, but—and this is important—*that did not mean the time spent looking at those houses was a waste or a failure*. If anything, the process taught me more about what I was looking for. I learned things about myself. I saw more options. Saying all those nos made me a more discerning buyer, so that when we saw the seventy-seventh house, we *knew* what we were saying yes to. So, too, "failed" dating relationships aren't necessarily failures. They provide vital information about who we are and who we're becoming, as well as who we might do well to *become* with.

If there are signs that make you feel you don't want to drive long-distance with that person, by all means take that information and thank God for it. That's okay. You can say a peaceful adieu to dating and be grateful for what you learned.

Perhaps the best advice I ever heard on breaking up came from my friend Scott. His counsel: "Just because you have two first-class people doesn't mean you'll have a first-class relationship." This truth-bomb made all the difference as I wrestled with a breakup early in my twenties, anxious that unless I could articulate what was wrong with *him* or wrong with *me*, we really should have been able to work things out. The need to blame or find fault in the wake of a breakup was strong. However, Scott's words gave me freedom to affirm that I could have tried my best, and he could have tried his best—and we could still esteem one another as great people in Christ—and yet we also could agree that dating each other wasn't bringing out the best in either of us. We just weren't a good fit, even if no one was particularly at fault. I had some girlfriends at the time who wanted to validate and encourage me after the breakup with comments such as "He didn't deserve you anyway," or "You dodged a bullet there," but such comfort is a double-edged knife. After all, dissing a brother in Christ is not the way we are to speak of each other in the family of God, even if our grievances are legitimate.

Relationships don't usually fail because *one* person has an irredeemable character flaw. People are more complex than that, and the way we talk about breakups can allow for more nuance. We all have deeply rooted character flaws. And we all have some really great qualities. Sometimes you can have two fabulous-but-flawed people who just bring out more flaw than fabulous in each other. Sometimes, two sinner-saints can make it work in dating. And sometimes, they know it's not the best idea to keep on going, and that's okay.

WHAT NOT TO ROAD TEST IN DATING

The whole point of dating is for us to assess how compatible a partnership we might forge with this person. Even without sexual intimacy, dating enables us to figure out whether we can talk with someone, work with them, laugh with them, play with them, and enjoy their company alone as well as in a larger group.

However, for all the practice we get at intimacy and partnership, dating remains a terrible time to test sexual compatibility. Sex is the one type of intimacy we don't need to road test in dating. What's more, the information we acquire wouldn't be reliable. Why? Because the experience and expectations of early-encounter forbidden sex is not an indicator of what a long-term, committed, covenantal intimacy would look and feel like. It's chalk and cheese. One hundred percent of the married couples I've asked agree their first kisses and first sex were *nothing* like what sex developed into years later. Research bears this out. In some of the most comprehensive studies ever done on sexual satisfaction, the National Survey of Sexual Health and Behavior reports that, contrary to the popular belief that singles are having more frequent and better sex, the data strongly favors marriage when it comes to long-term sexual satisfaction. "Want more and better sex?" ask relationship experts Linda and Charlie Bloom in their survey of the research.[5] "Get married and stay married."

When sharing this data with college students, I try to break it down with the most accessible examples I can think of. "What this means," I tell them, "is that it's not the football quarterback, or the porn star, or the winner of the *Bachelor* with the abs of steel who is having the best sex. What it means is that the people in your life most qualified to give advice on how to have really great, satisfying sex might well be . . . your parents." It's a horrifying moment for most of the audience, but the point is memorably made: early sex and premarital sex don't give you good feedback on chemistry, compatibility, and the odds of long-term sexual satisfaction. If your parents are still married, they are likely to

> SEX IS THE ONE TYPE OF INTIMACY WE DON'T NEED TO ROAD TEST IN DATING.

have racked up hundreds—if not thousands—of more satisfying sexual encounters than any of the studs overheard bragging in the locker room. Marriage, as it turns out, is a brilliant environment for fine-tuning sexual compatibility. Dating? Not so much.

But while dating is a bad time to test sexual compatibility, it is a superb opportunity to test sexual integrity. Dating gives us multiple opportunities to learn how to faithfully steward our bodies, our relationships, and our desires in ways that set us up for long-term intimacy, even as we're evaluating whether we'd like to spend the rest of our lives with this person as our copilot.

A sibling mind-set can both guard and guide us in the dating process. It can help lessen the anxiety of "first contact" when we're getting to know someone; it can help us handle sexual temptation while dating as we keep our Christian brother or sister's godliness in mind; and finally, if the relationship doesn't work out, it can help us navigate breakups better knowing that the end of dating doesn't mean the end of the relationship altogether.

Two things remain clear: whether we're considering dating, in the euphoria of it, or recovering from a breakup, remembering we're family in Christ anchors us. And second, no matter which stage of relationship we're in, we are called to sexual integrity; and it is that conversation which leads us to our final chapter.

CHAPTER 9

WHERE DO WE GO FROM HERE?

SEXUAL STEWARDSHIP AS A PRACTICE AND AN INVITATION

Out of five women on stage, Donna was the last person on the panel I expected to answer the hot-button question. "How do I handle feelings of sexual desire if I'm not married?" asked an earnest young woman. All eyes in the room turned to the youth pastor panelist, expecting a well-rehearsed answer about masturbation. But it was Donna—widowed and in her sixties—who leaned forward and reached for the microphone.

"That's something I'm wrestling with too," she said to the you-could-hear-a-pin-drop quiet room. "While I was married, there was obviously a lot of opportunity to express and satisfy sexual desire, and yet there were also times when travel or illness meant we didn't. Now that Juan is gone, I still have those longings. That part of me didn't die when he did. Being a widow doesn't mean I'm half a woman. This might be a new situation, but the same principles apply: I still need to be faithful in what I do with sexual feelings. So now I'm actively seeking out a variety of ways to experience joy and connection in my body given that sex isn't an option. I'm the first one on the dance floor at weddings. I hug people. I volunteer in the church nursery so I can get more of the cuddles I crave. And I talk to God about it a great deal, because there are some deep needs of being seen and known that only he can really fill now."

In thirty seconds, Donna tapped into the heart of the issue: sexuality and sexual feelings don't belong exclusively to the married. Christian men and women of all ages and stages in life experience longings for connection and touch, and there will always be healthy ways for us to meet those needs, as well as temptations for us to meet them in dangerous ways. Donna's answer also illustrates how sexuality and desire is a *human issue*—not just a young adult issue—and as such, it calls for lifelong sexual fidelity appropriate to whatever stage we're in.

STEWARDSHIP VS. CAUTION TAPE

The word "stewardship" has long been used in Christian circles for how we handle money and, in recent years, for how we relate to creation. *Merriam-Webster* defines stewardship as "the conducting, supervising, or managing of something," most often "the careful and responsible management of something entrusted to one's care."[1] The underlying assumption is that we steward things we consider valuable. We steward time and money because they're limited resources. We steward creation because God made it, we live interdependently with it, and our future depends on it. Resources such as these are not just common things; they're precious assets.

If we take the view that God created maleness and femaleness, sexuality can rightly be seen as a gift and a resource, and as such the best word for how we handle it is *stewardship*. We don't just *manage* our sexuality as if it were a pesky problem, nor do we seek to *control* it as a risk and danger. Sexuality is a gift. It needs more than caution tape and control—it needs stewarding. As with all precious resources, sexuality can be abused and misused, but our default position toward it requires acknowledging its value and preciousness.

Moreover, sexuality—the ability and desire to connect as men and women—is something everybody has from birth. Sexuality isn't acquired or activated by marriage; it's innate. This means that everyone needs to think about how to steward their sexuality in whatever stage of life they're in. Just as it's not only the rich who need to think about stewarding money—for the love of money can be a root of evil to poor and rich alike (1 Timothy 6:10)—it's not just the young and restless who need to think about stewarding sexuality. We all do. No one is exempt from the task of figuring out how to put sex and sexuality in their proper places. It's a worthy task, with an eye-roller of a name.

> SEXUALITY IS A GIFT. IT NEEDS MORE THAN CAUTION TAPE AND CONTROL—IT NEEDS STEWARDING.

IT BEGINS WITH "CH" AND
RHYMES WITH "ZASTITY"

Christians have long talked about *abstinence* as being central to sexual faithfulness, but that isn't nearly a big enough word for what it means to steward sexuality. The bigger word we're looking for is *chastity*. As author Marlena Graves observed, "Evangelicals, like most of the world, are obsessed with sex. We talk about avoiding premarital sex and other sorts of sexual immorality, but we're not very good at knowing how to embrace a chaste life."[2] Abstinence (which means refraining from sex) and celibacy (which means a commitment not to marry, and thus not have sex) are subsets of the much bigger concept of *chastity* (which is a commitment to keeping sex and sexuality in their proper places).[3]

Chastity has gotten a pretty bad rap. The image that comes to mind is a medieval chastity belt—a clunky iron symbol of paranoia over female sexuality. But chastity deserves a chance to redeem its reputation. Far from seeking to suppress sexuality, chastity—rightly understood—is far more about acknowledging the value and power of sexuality and focusing its energy on committed relationships within our community.[4] As Graves noted, "We need more conversation about what it means . . . to love another person instead of all this talk about 'avoidance.' . . . How do we honor God with our bodies and in our communities while seeking the flourishing—and not the destruction or manipulation and control—of another?"[5]

This book is an invitation to open up more of these kinds of conversations about what it might look like to show love and build relationships in *embodied*, *gendered* and yet *holy*, *healthy*, *chaste* ways as befits the family of God. The reigning cultural view that "sex is okay as long as people don't get hurt" (or at least as long as your intentions are honest), falls far short of God's good intentions for sex, sexuality, and our bodies. And yet, to talk about *chastity* as an alternative to this seems out of touch at best and, to many, just plain impossible. Yet, properly understood, chastity includes the possibility of Song of Songs erotica: it's about having sex and sexuality in their good, God-ordained places of gift and flourishing.

As Lauren Winner put it: "If we see scripture not merely as a code of behavior but as a map of God's reality, and if we take seriously the pastoral task of helping Christians live chastely, the church needs not merely to recite decontextualized Bible verses, but to ground our ethic in the faithful living of the fullness of the gospel."[6] Scripture has a good story to tell about sexuality and intimacy, if only we'd immerse ourselves in it.

The *Catechism of the Catholic Church* helpfully explained why sexual stewardship in the form of chastity must be part of our "faithful living of the fullness of the gospel." It described chastity as "the successful integration of sexuality within the person and thus the inner unity of man in his bodily and spiritual being. Sexuality, in which man's belonging to the bodily and biological world is expressed, becomes personal and truly human when it is integrated into the relationship of one person to another."[7] In other words, chastity describes how we faithfully express our identity, as both spiritual and sexual beings, through how we relate to God and those around us. We do not love God and our neighbors as disembodied beings. Our response to the gospel is an embodied one—Jesus calls our *whole* selves to be part of his body. We are to offer our bodies to God as our reasonable act of worship, and our sexual identity and behavior is inextricably linked with that call (Romans 12:1).

IT'S FOR EVERYONE

We can't talk about Christian discipleship, then, without talking about chastity and sexual faithfulness. What we do in and with our bodies is integral to our existence as spiritual beings. The pressures of our sex-mad world combined with the needs, desires, and feelings we experience in our bodies mean we need more than the wafer-thin theology offered by dos and don'ts. We need what Bible scholars call "thick theologies" to give us a solid framework for knowing how the truth of our life with God through Christ impacts every area of our day-to-day life.

Slogans such as "true love waits" are not enough. They're about as helpful as giving someone a tent and then wishing them well as they set out to spend decades in the wilderness. To bear the weight of the sexual questions and pressures laid on us, we need a more robust, all-weather structure—a scriptural steel framework, deeply anchored in the solid foundations of grace. We need a theology that acknowledges all the things our bodies, souls, and spirits long for, and does not try to shame those desires into silence. We need a theology that acknowledges we were made for community and relationship with other men and women, and shows us a way to express and experience that in healthy, familial ways.

Talking about chastity—or sexual stewardship, if that phrase is easier to relate to—means we acknowledge that our sexuality really exists, and that it has real power and real value. And, because we recognize its power and value, we take active steps to guard and guide it. The teen experiencing a dizzying rush of hormones and sexual awareness needs to hear voices within the family of God telling them they're not a freak to feel the way they do, that God made bodies to feel things and we need not be ashamed of it. We need mentors encouraging them to name and acknowledge those feelings, and then consider the accompanying responsibility.

Couples who are dating need more than just a "don't have sex" message from their spiritual communities. They need conversation that acknowledges it's normal to feel blindsided by the surge of desire that might accompany a kiss. The electric jolt that can accompany physical chemistry is part of how God made us—it's what Song of Songs (and much of Spotify's music) is about! There are smart ways and dumb ways to deal with high-voltage currents in this life. If we teach our kids about electricity in our homes, we can teach them about electricity in our bodies too. God created that spark, and we needn't deny it or hide from it.

And, as we've already acknowledged, sexual stewardship is not just a conversation for the young. Marlena Graves elaborated on some of the challenges faced by older singles, such as Donna from the beginning of this chapter, who have lost a spouse and still long for companionship:

> The problem is—if they remarry, many will lose their income. So they may be sexually monogamous (or not) but they don't marry because they don't want to lose Social Security income . . . or survivor benefits from their deceased spouse's pension. Or, they don't want to upend family dynamics by remarrying late in life. . . . So in order to avoid a huge family debacle, the elderly remain unmarried, cohabitate, or they live in separate residences but engage in sexual activity.[8]

Unlike Donna, many widows and widowers do not have a game plan for finding the community they crave and tending to their need for touch. "The elderly," observed Graves, "are not practiced in abstinence and chastity" either, and need discipleship on stewarding their longings in God-honoring ways.

It does us no good to deny that people of all ages and in all stages have sexual feelings. Nor does it help those who express sexual longing to respond, "Well, just don't feel that way." People *do* feel those feelings, and we can learn to see both our sexuality and our legitimate desires for relationship and intimacy as cues and invitations to press deeper into community. This is true for all ages, marital stages, and sexual orientations. Consider Wesley Hill's convictions on how to faithfully live as a gay, celibate Christian:

> Rather than interpreting my sexuality as a license to go to bed with someone or even to form a monogamous sexual partnership with him, I can harness and guide its energies in the direction of sexually abstinent, yet intimate, friendship. . . . Being gay can lead to being chaste, just as being straight can. . . . We hear so much about the hookup culture and various other forms of promiscuity among straight people, but heterosexuality can just as well be expressed in chivalry or even celibacy. And something parallel is true for gay people. My being gay and saying no to gay sex may lead me to be *more* of a friend to men, not less.[9]

I'm a married, straight woman, and I say a hearty amen to the wisdom of this celibate, gay brother in Christ. Even if our experience of sexual attraction and marriage is vastly different, we share the same thick theology of sexual stewardship. We acknowledge our creation as sexual beings. We acknowledge our longing for community and relationship as a good, central part of being human. We do not see our sexuality as an obstacle or enemy to building community, but as something which—if faithfully stewarded—is central to it. And we do not see chastity as just for the single and hormone-flooded, but as relevant to the faith and practice of believers of all ages.

A PRACTICE, NOT A RULE

Have you ever wondered why we use the word "practice" to describe the professional work of doctors and lawyers, both of whom are required to spend years studying and getting qualified? For someone like me who always thought practice was something one did as preparation, it seemed counterintuitive. However, practice can speak to more than the idea of preparation. Practice also refers to what the dictionary describes as "the actual application or use of an idea, belief or method, as opposed to theories relating to it." So, after many years of medical school or law school studying theories, doctors and lawyers *practice* when they finally get to apply what they've learned to healing patients and serving clients.

Chastity is not just something we practice (by remaining abstinent as we prepare for marriage) until we graduate on our wedding night. It is better understood in the second sense of the word "practice": a rhythm, a discipline, a way of applying our faith for the rest of our lives, rather than just reading about it. It's not something we ever perfect or get past, because sexual faithfulness is a lifelong discipline, regardless of age, marital status, or attractions. For the unmarried, practicing chastity means committing to abstinence and finding healthy, appropriate ways to love and be loved within the family of God. For the married, practicing chastity means not having sex with anyone other than your spouse, and sometimes it may mean having sex with your spouse when you don't feel like it (1 Corinthians 7:1–4), as well as cultivating holy, rich relationships with the men and women around us. Whether we are married or unmarried, younger or older, straight or gay, God calls us to practice chastity. Each of us is to honor and steward our sexuality, seeking healthy, appropriate ways to show and receive love within the beautiful, big family of God.

IT TAKES A VILLAGE

Whenever I travel, people who know I work from home ask who is taking care of my kids in my absence. I almost always reply that this or that person from church is helping out. "It takes a village," I reply, which is shorthand for "some things are too big to tackle alone." We need the support and encouragement of a broader community.

Child-rearing is definitely one of those areas where we need other people, and so is sexual discipleship. Sex and sexuality may be personal issues, but they are not private: we live out our maleness and femaleness in every relationship. When it comes to disciplining our sexual desires and stewarding our sexuality, it really helps to have a village. In particular, we need a village who *talks* to each other about these things, rather than just *assumes* we're all on the same page. If we are silent or constantly cryptic about sex, we effectively leave our thirsty church family to drink the cultural waters we're swimming in, rather than providing living water. Our sexual values and imaginations are continually being shaped and discipled by *something* or *someone*, and on our own we have little help in filtering and processing those influences. If we don't want our sex-ed teachers to be Snapchat and Hollywood, our villages need to be intentional about leading the conversation.

DEVELOP A SHARED VISION

We need to be investing in becoming communities who speak well of singleness, sexuality, and chastity, and actively resist the idolization of marriage and the nuclear family.[10] We need conversations and curriculum with a bigger vision for living as brothers and sisters in Christ. It does me no good to be ready to love and be loved as a sister in Christ if I walk into a room where everyone believes married women should only be friends with other women. I can't build a family mind-set alone. Other people have to share this vision for the church as family to make it work. It takes a village.

And by contrast, it would make all the difference in the world to my unmarried friends—who are grappling with dating and sex, or who are solo parenting, or who wish they could be parenting—to know that there is a community of men and women rooting for them, and they will not be alone *no matter what* their marital status may be. One beautiful way I've seen this happen was on a short-term missions team co-led by a capable, godly unmarried woman, and a married man. We publicly honored and prayed for these two as they led a team that included another married couple and believers of different ages to serve a partner ministry in Honduras. They were a family delegation of chaste brothers and sisters.

"One of the best ways Christian communities can support

chastity," suggested Lauren Winner, "is to ensure that married people and single folks are in relationship with each other."[11] Fostering relationships between married and single people means being intentional about inviting people to eat meals or go to the ball game or to the farmer's market. It means inviting your married friend to the Bunco or poker night, or inviting your unmarried friend to your kids' Christmas pageant. It means adding odd numbers of chairs to the Thanksgiving table and taking a look around church on a Sunday after the service to see if anyone has been left out of the lunch invites.

ASK THE HARD QUESTIONS

Fostering a community that helps one another with chastity goes further than extending invitations though. It also means being willing to ask my single, dating friends hard questions that require more than vague, dismissive answers. Many a friend has shared that knowing someone loved them enough to ask what they did on that date has done much to help them make better choices with their sexuality.

What's more, it's important to note that the support is not just one-directional, with the married looking out for the unmarried. Fostering sexually disciplined communities means the married also need to be willing to trust the unmarried enough to share their life and struggles. I have some incredibly wise friends who may not be married but know a great deal about perseverance, patience, celebration, prayer, and a number of other things I need to learn and practice in my own marriage.

Community-level discipleship means we seek out relationships to discuss and debrief what we're reading and watching, and it means being honest about the questions and desires these stir in us. I've worried, for example, about the influence some television shows, such as *Game of Thrones* and *Outlander*, might have on my husband and me. Talking with other believing friends—not so much about the shows themselves, but the impact of the shows on our own sexual imaginations—has done much to help us process these concerns. Sometimes the simple act of naming the things that interest, confuse, or entice us can play a significant role in deflating their power over us.

BE BIBLICALLY POSITIVE ABOUT SEX

Perhaps one of the biggest ways our community—the family of God—can help us practice chastity is by building habits of better, biblical ways of thinking and talking about sex, sexuality, and intimacy.

The church, for all its many advantages, has historically had a less than positive attitude toward sex. However, Jesus and the witness of Scripture are overwhelmingly positive toward sexuality, strongly rebuking ascetic alternatives. "Do not deprive one another," wrote Paul to the married, and "it is better to marry than to burn with passion" to the sexually frustrated unmarried (1 Corinthians 7:5, 9). Paul is plainly pro-sex here. "Rejoice in the wife of your youth," enjoined the teacher in Proverbs 5:18. It's precisely because sex and sexuality are viewed as God's good gifts that the veto on extramarital sex is given in the first place. Nobody bothers to fence in a wasteland: we only cordon off valuable property we're afraid will get trampled. We protect what we prize, and Scripture's protections around sexuality point to the positive, precious gift it is, denouncing "any behavior which breaks the links between sex, personhood and relationship."[12]

We help one another to live chastely by reminding one

another of the *good* we're celebrating, and thus protecting. We have a biblical mandate and invitation to enjoy sex, maleness, femaleness, and fully embodied living. When asked, "What does the Bible say about sex?" it would be wonderful to have a generation of believers who answer not with the knee-jerk response, "Don't do it!" but enthusiastically reply, "God made it, and it's *good*!" A direct application of honoring the goodness of sex within marriage would be protecting its boundaries, but it would so help us if we could reframe our conversations about sexuality in ways that honor it as God's good gift—even to the unmarried!—rather than something to remain hidden and undiscussed. Honest, body-positive conversation about sexuality belongs in the church, not just at the Red Table. Our village needs to find its voice; we can't walk the walk unless we talk the talk first.

USE YOUR WORDS: REWIRE YOUR BRAIN FOR LOVE

I would be hard-pressed to remember most of the classes I took in college, but one is particularly deeply etched into my memory. The few months I spent in Political Discourse Analysis opened up to me the fascinating world of neurolinguistic programming, which is a fancy way of describing how language creates pathways in the brain. Our class assignment was to read early historical documents from settlers in South Africa and note the words they used to describe the indigenous population. We were then asked to trace how the choice of certain *words* shaped how a generation of settlers *thought* about (and thus *treated*) those people. South Africa's apartheid legacy of racial discrimination can be directly traced through generations of people who'd been taught by language to see native people as "other" and "lesser."[13] I'd never realized that the words communities used so deeply affected the way they thought, and thus behaved.

Our brains are affected by our word choices, for better or for worse. The Guugu Yimithirr tribe in Australia offers a stellar example with their off-the-charts spatial abilities. Guugu Yimithirr kids as young as five can accurately tell you whether you're facing north or west without batting an eyelid (much less whipping out a compass). Why? In their native language, rather than use prepositions to describe how things relate to one another, they speak to each other in directions. Instead of saying, "Please step to the left," a tribe member might say, "Please step to the east." The result? A community with an internal compass imprinted by language.[14]

That language shapes how we think is true at the level of intimate relationships too. "What do you call your spouse?" is a common question in couples' counseling. A husband who regularly refers to his wife as "my love" or "my better half" is linguistically wiring his brain to see her as beloved. His word choice sets him up for a much more joyful relationship with his wife than that of the husband who, even jokingly, refers to his wife as "my ball and chain." Philosopher Donald Schön coined the phrase "generative metaphor" to describe how our mental and verbal images play out contextually.[15] For example, a company described as "fragmented" might be more likely to hire a job candidate who talks about seeking "integrative solutions." And a husband who describes his wife as something only found in ancient prisons might be more likely to experience his marriage as restrictive.

There are two language shifts we can make as the church to help rewire our brains toward healthier thinking. One is for us to continue to explain and reclaim the depth and breadth of what "love" means. Our sex-saturated world is longing for love and connection, and the Scriptures provide a rich treasure of loves that go further and deeper than our old friend *eros* can. Speaking often and well of the unconditional, covenantal *agape* love, with which God loves us and calls us to love one another, is a deep balm for our lonely, insecure souls. Our hearts long to know such a love exists, and we need to hear it spoken of. We also need to deeply honor friendship (*phileo*) and loyalty (*storge*). Even if one's life is sexless, there is no reason it need be loveless.

Love has many textures and tones, and we would do well to re-story our communities accordingly. What's more, growing in our appreciation for the other "loves" will help us put sexual love into its proper place, for "the Bible does not teach that *agape* supplants erotic love. But it does teach very clearly that the erotic finds its fulfilment only in the context of *agape*."[16]

The second language shift that can help move our communities toward deeper intimacy as well as chastity is to focus on the language of *family*, which Krish Kandiah suggested would have "huge implications, not just for our own personal spiritual development but for our understanding of mission, evangelism, worship, justice, hospitality, and discipleship." Instead of talking about "going to church" as a place where we receive religious goods and services (we speak of "church shopping," for example), we could talk about "being the church."[17] If *family* were our generative metaphor, and we increasingly spoke about church as the "household of God," it would radically reorient the way we thought, and thus behaved, toward each other.

I was recently asked if I would do the announcements at our Sunday morning worship service. Announcements can sometimes seem like the necessary evil of corporate worship: boring, but we can't do without them. I'd spent much of the Saturday prior figuring out our family calendar for the months ahead, and so I decided to continue in that mind-set for church announcements.

"Good morning, church family!" I greeted. "It's a busy season in everybody's households, and so in order to help us all stay on the same page, this morning we're going to call the announcements what they really are: family calendaring. These are some things coming up in church life you need to take note of, because you know what they say, 'The family that prays together . . . calendars together.'" This got a big laugh from the congregation, but better than that, it focused their attention. They weren't being given take-it-or-leave-it information as if it were a leaflet left on their windshield in a parking lot; they were being invited to participate in the everyday intimacy of family living.

As Kandiah explained, "When family is used as a generative metaphor for church, it can transform not only our preconceptions and expectations of church, but also our preconceptions and expectations of family." [18] This has absolutely been true for me. The more aware I've become of family language in the Bible, the more profoundly my experience of church has changed. I see communion as a family meal, and worship as communication with our Father based in adoptive love rather than on effort. And more and more, family language helps me to see fellow believers as the brothers and sisters they are. I don't get to pick and choose with whom I will be in relationship—in Christ, I'm in relationship with *everyone*, and will be for eternity. The men and women around me aren't temptations to be avoided or annoyances to be endured, but people to be loved. And my nuclear family can—and must—find its place within this bigger family of God.

A WINSOME PICTURE OF THE GOSPEL

Perhaps the most thrilling aspect of this shift in perspective is the impact it can have on the world. This bigger vision of the church as a "non-nuclear, welcoming, and diverse family can make the difference to all sorts of vulnerable people and model to an increasingly divided and isolated world a glimpse into the coming kingdom of God."[19] The more we speak about church as a family to whom we belong, the more we will think and live that out, which is itself a *powerful witness* and *invitation* to a world craving connection and belonging. "In my Father's house are many rooms," said Jesus (John 14:2). Oh, that we would speak, think, and live in a way that invites the world to move in as one of his beloved children too.

By shifting our language to be more in line with the Bible's emphasis on the church as a family who loves one another well, we get to portray a beautiful picture of the gospel. The world is supposed to know we are Christians by our love. By adopting language and practices that show Christian men and women in deep, close, holy love relationships, we model something powerful to the world. God's sexual ethic and pattern for relationship is *good news* to us. His invitation to live as sons and daughters in his family is a promise of *abundant life*. If people have heard that the Christian life is prudish, disembodied, and sexually repressed, we have either badly communicated the message or shown that we have terribly misunderstood it ourselves. The Bible speaks of maleness and femaleness with joy. It speaks of intimate community as a reality. It speaks of sex as a gift. Our witness should bear that out.

The world around us is aching for authentic sexuality and fulfilling relationships, and as brothers and sisters in Christ, we have something to offer. Believers have something better to say about being men and women than the prevailing cultural scripts. We know something deeper and more profound about love than *Love Actually*. We have something better than "wishful thinking." We have *hope* as our anchor. This may be a book about healthy relationships between men and women in the

> **CHRISTIAN MEN AND WOMEN IN DEEP, CLOSE, HOLY LOVE RELATIONSHIPS MODEL SOMETHING POWERFUL TO THE WORLD.**

family of God, but there is an evangelistic silver lining to all this, for as we live out what it means to be the family of God in every area of our lives—including our sexual formation—the world cannot fail to notice.

We are called to be familiar with each other, and to love one another deeply and well as part of God's family. And we can all invite more guests. The intimacy of God's family is available for everyone.

TRIP OVERVIEW

FROM SIDE HUGS TO A HOLY KISS

It was February, and from the warmth of my California kitchen I watched the weather forecasts with alarm. I was heading into a polar vortex that weekend, with predicted temperatures of -30 degrees Fahrenheit and wind chill factors below -50. I was shivering in California, where it was currently above 50 degrees. I had no idea how I'd cope with a 100-degree drop in temperature. It's no understatement to say I was terrified of winter in Minnesota.

I've lived my entire life in sunny places: South Africa and then California. I was in my twenties the first time I saw snow, and the sensation of walking on something with *depth* was unlike anything I'd experienced before. I had no experience shoveling snow, walking on ice, or driving in frozen conditions. And to make my anxiety worse, dear church friends of ours had narrowly survived a terrible car wreck a month prior when they'd hit black ice and flipped their vehicle while driving in Utah. I had no idea how I'd survive three weeks in a frozen tundra. I invested in wool base layers. I researched how I could possibly get around without once having to drive.

A week into my stay, I confessed my fears of winter to a local Minnesotan. He laughed. "Why were you so afraid?" he asked, gesturing to the indoor thermostat set at a constant 70 degrees. I explained, adding that I'd watched the YouTube video on how to walk safely on the ice "like a penguin" several times now, shuffling with feet close together, eyes up, and arms slightly apart. On a campus with thousands of students who all seemed to be walking around normally, you could easily pick me out as the one with the distinctively "penguinish" gait.

"That's fair," he conceded. I was right to be concerned. The risks are real, and his relative confidence in navigating snow was based on a lifetime's experience in identifying the danger signs of cold weather. It had been a long time since he'd worried about ice: he just generally knew when to proceed with extra caution. He knew how to bundle up and what to look out for. For him, the snowy landscape was magnificent more than it was menacing. California rookie that I was, I needed to go a lot more slowly. Did I wanna build a snowman? That sounded fun, but impossible. I wasn't ready to play yet. I still had to proceed with caution.

HERE BE DRAGONS

The invitation for us to develop meaningful gendered relationships might sound like the threat of a midwestern winter. If we've had no experience in navigating those conditions, and we've heard horror stories of the dangers of whiteouts and black ice, the thought of stepping out into unfamiliar terrain is rightly frightening. In the words of ancient cartographers who wrote warnings to indicate unexplored areas of the sea, "Here be dragons." Who knew what lay beyond the borders of the known? It might be treacherous.

I may have been rightly cautious of driving in subzero temperatures, but with a little practice, it became doable and even enjoyable. There is a wild, quiet beauty to the winter palette, and it was mine to discover once I recalibrated my fears.

When it comes to male-female relationships in the church, I'd say my fear setting is probably similar to that of a Minnesotan who grew up in the snow. I've been getting around comfortably in these conditions for some time now, and for the most part I can carry on as usual, relying on my experience radar to let me know when I need to exercise extra caution.

I understand that this invitation into deeper relationships with brothers and sisters may seem as terrifying as navigating ice was to me. But I also have confidence that once we get in there and start moving around, we'll acclimate and find our way. My first few days of tentative shuffling gave way to a growing joy in walking in the silence of snow, and by the end of a month, I drove a couple of hours in frigid conditions without a single panicked moment. However, I still drove with caution. People still slip and fall. Drivers still have accidents. But that doesn't mean we should never leave the house, never engage in community, and never explore the landscape. With a little practice, the right gear, a healthy assessment of our own limits, and an eye on the changing atmospheric conditions, it really is possible to get out there and enjoy.

I DON'T KNOW WHAT YOU'RE TALKING ABOUT

One of the first people I met in Minnesota was a joyful gray-haired woman named Mary. We found ourselves in a lunch line together, and she asked what I was working on. I explained the premise of this book, hoping to somehow offer a breezy, not-too-intense, slightly funny elevator pitch about exploring the theology of family as a counternarrative to our sex-crazed age—all before we reached the buffet table.

I watched her face closely, trying to read whether she was following me. She stared at me blank-faced, and I felt a rising panic. What if I couldn't explain what this book was about? What if the premise of the book was *all wrong*? I tried again using different words, a different angle. We were nearly at the dinner rolls; time was running out. She stared at me a little while longer, then said as gently as she could, "I'm sorry, but I don't know what you're talking about."

As we sat down to lunch, she explained. Did I realize she was a nun? Perhaps her purple sparkly hoodie had thrown me off, she said, explaining that she'd taken holy orders with the Sisters of Charity decades ago, and pointing to the ring on her finger, which I'd mistaken for a wedding ring. All of a sudden, her confusion made total sense. I was describing a church landscape fraught with sexual tension, where we have little to no sense of what it is to develop community informed by our identity as brothers and sisters. Mary's lifelong experience was exactly the opposite. She'd spent her life as a sister, in the company and partnership of other brothers and sisters with her order. She hadn't had to ward off a mixed signal for decades. She was quite categorically *not* the target audience for my book. She was the equivalent of an Inuit in my Minnesota winter example: born and raised in the snow, and not the least bit afraid of arctic winds.

This book is not for the Marys of this world, whose entire lives have been framed by living as brothers and sisters in Christ. This book is for the Bronwyns in Minnesota: those afraid to even step outside for fear of getting hurt. It's an invitation to intimacy for those who've been lonely inside for too long.

FROM SIDE HUGS TO A HOLY KISS

"Greet one another with a holy kiss," instructed the apostle Paul in his second letter to the church at Corinth (2 Corinthians 13:12). This wording is retained in almost all modern translations, with J. B. Philips being a notable exception in his rendering, "A handshake all round, please!" What did Paul mean by a "holy kiss"? The awkward side hug of modern Christianity doesn't quite cut it. A pastor friend of mine has opted for a fist bump as his chosen greeting: a gesture that always makes me feel loved and old at the same time.

> WE NEED TO RECLAIM THE GROUND BETWEEN THE AWKWARD SIDE HUG AND GREETING EACH OTHER WITH A HOLY KISS, WHATEVER THAT MIGHT MEAN IN OUR CONTEXT.

Throughout this book, my intention has been to show that Scripture invites us to express familial affection in Christ in holy and wholly appropriate ways. Somehow we need to reclaim the ground between the awkward side hug and greeting each other with a holy kiss, whatever that might mean in our context. Whether it's a kiss or a hug or a warm handshake or a fist bump is not really the point. (Remember my awkward handholding with Karabo? These signals have cultural context.) Paul was encouraging those in the church to express affection for one another, physically and publicly. The warm, close relationships between believing brothers and sisters were to be celebrated and nurtured as they pursued holiness in community. Family closeness was part of church life and the regular rhythms of worship.

Marriages can thrive rather than be threatened by such a network of healthy relationships. Unmarried believers can find connection and closeness by this experience of family. Gendered relationships don't have to be sexual to be emotionally and spiritually enriching.

It doesn't have to be weird. It can be wonderful.

ACKNOWLEDGMENTS

Just as it takes a village to raise a kid or to nurture a culture of healthy sexual discipleship, so, too, it takes a village to bring a book into the world. More and more I understand Paul's overcome-with-gratitude attitude writing to his church family in Philippians 1:3: "I thank my God every time I remember you." Even on my most organized, motivated, and highly caffeinated day, I would not have been able to pull this off on my own. I thank my God every time I remember you:

Ruth Samsel, for taking a chance on me and believing this idea was worth turning into a book proposal. And Bill Jensen, for graciously stepping in to represent me.

Jessica Wong, Christine Anderson, Brigitta Nortker, and Natalie Nyquist—the amazing editors who put Spanx on my words and pulled this book into much better shape! To Aryn Van Dyke, Rachel Tockstein, Shea Nolan, Jamie Lockard, Karen Campbell, and the rest of the amazing team at Thomas Nelson with endless patience figuring out the cover and brainstorming how we could best reach and serve the church through this project. You were an encouragement and example to me throughout, y'all are the dream team.

The amazing women of Redbud Writers Guild, an incredible community in which to grow as a writer. I am grateful to Leslie Leyland Fields, Janna Northrup, Lee Wolfe Blum, and Dorothy Greco for their unflagging support and insightful questions as I worked on chapters in the Minnesota winter.

Aleah Marsden, Jen Michel, Liz Ditty, and Tina Osterhouse: Redbuds, writing sisters, and cheerleaders in gritty commitment. You are such amazing writers and even better friends. I thank God I had you all to witness me clicking *send* on this manuscript (and every stage in between!).

The Collegeville Institute, for the invitation to be a residential scholar and work on this book for a blissfully uninterrupted three weeks. What a gift.

Alastair Roberts, Hannah Anderson, April Fiet, Graham Ware, Hannah Malcolm, and the other partners in the Saltshaker Blog project: for modeling how a brother-sister mindset could give us a framework to talk about divisive issues without dividing.

Aimee Byrd, Tim Fall, Lore Wilbert, Kelley Mathews, Steve Wiens, Dan Brennan, Katelyn Beaty, and Karen Swallow Prior: thank you for hosting gracious conversations in the public sphere on these topics with grace, truth, and clarity.

My just-a-text-away girlfriends, whose encouragement and gifs have picked me up off the floor more times than I can count. Wriderleas, Octopus-emoji-senders, G, cucumber-field-lovers, fun-hat-wearers, book club: you know who you are. Thank you for laughter and Kleenexes.

Dan Seitz and Stanford Gibson, *adelphoi* and *philoi*. Thank you for developing the thoughts behind this book over years of conversation. It wouldn't exist without you.

Christine Caine and the incredible team at Propel Women, for the invitation to partner in kingdom work in so many ways. I am so grateful God connected us.

My church family at FBC Davis, who have embodied what it means to live as brothers and sisters to us so often and in so many ways. Thank you for loving us. Thank you for loving our children. To College Life, for the privilege of living life with you during your college years. To our home group, for the week by week witness of life together. To the pastoral staff: it is such a joy to work alongside you and learn from you.

Ray and Wendy Rodriguez, who have prayed a thousand prayers for us and eaten a thousand meals with us over the years. I can't even imagine what our lives would be like without you welcoming us into your fold, treating us as your son and daughter, and our kids as yours too. La familia.

To my parents, Corinne Hudson and Michael Marriott, for decades of love and encouragement. I am so grateful for the constancy of your support, even when separated by continents! To my seesters, Faye Marriott and Taryn Houlsby: I love you. Your eyeballs are staring at me.

To my husband, Jeremy. Best of neighbors, closest of friends, brother in Christ, and beloved husband. You are the kindest and most gentle man I know, and I am so thankful to be your wife. Thank you for your steadiness when I freak out, and for making space for me to write. To our kids, Tegwyn, Callum, and Declan: thank you for making me laugh every single day, and for celebrating every milestone of this book with cheers and dance parties. I've been telling you this since the day you were born and I'll say it again here: I'm so thankful God gave us you.

A non-awkward side hug for all of you, my beloved readers.

ACKNOWLEDGMENTS

And finally, to my God, whose love as a Father compelled you to send Jesus so we could be part of your family, and whose Spirit has been my companion and counselor every step of the way: all praise and honor and thanks go to you.

NOTES

CHAPTER 1: AWKWARD, LONELY, AND OVERSEXED

1. Christopher Ash, *Marriage: Sex in the Service of God* (Leicester: InterVarsity Press, 2003).

2. Jonathan Grant summarizes the core shifts of the past fifty years this way: "Four moral changes that took place among young people especially: the resurgence of the idea of sex as good in itself (witness Freud); the new ideal in which men and women would come together in sex as equal partners free of gender roles; a widespread view of sex as liberation from authority; and a new insistence that sexuality was a core part of individual identity." *Divine Sex: A Compelling Vision for Christian Relationships in a Hypersexualized Age* (Grand Rapids, MI: Brazos Press, 2015), 37.

3. Helen Fisher, "This Is Your Brain on Sex," interview by Krista Tippett, *On Being*, last updated April 5, 2018, https://onbeing .org/programs/helen-fisher-this-is-your-brain-on-sex-apr2017/.

4. David Foster Wallace, "Plain Old Untrendy Troubles and Emotions," *Guardian*, September 19, 2008, https://www .theguardian.com/books/2008/sep/20/fiction.

5. James K. A. Smith, *Desiring the Kingdom: Worship, Worldview, and Cultural Formation* (Grand Rapids, MI: Baker Academic, 2009), 40.

6. Andy Rau, "The Top 100 Most Read Bible Verses," Bible

Gateway, May 15, 2009, https://biblegateway.com/blog/2009/005/the-100-most-read-bible-verses-at-biblegatewaycom/.

7. Jen Wilkin, "3 Female Ghosts That Haunt the Church," Gospel Coalition, February 12, 2015, http://www.thegospelcoalition.org/article/3-female.

8. Dan Brennan, *Sacred Unions, Sacred Passions: Engaging the Mystery of Friendship Between Men and Women* (Elgin, IL: Faith Dance Publishing, 2010), 56–57.

9. Brennan, *Sacred Unions, Sacred Passions*, 56.

CHAPTER 2: UNASHAMED, MALE AND FEMALE

1. It is beyond the scope of this book to do anything more than acknowledge that gender dysphoria—the distress a person experiences as a result of the sex or gender they were assigned at birth—exists and deserves respectful and compassionate conversation. An early sense that your sex/gender is not who you really are is so painful precisely because sexuality is so central to our identity. For further reading, see Mark A. Yarhouse's books *Understanding Sexual Identity: A Resource for Youth Ministry* (Grand Rapids, MI: Zondervan, 2013) and *Understanding Gender Dysphoria: Navigating Transgender Issues in a Changing Culture* (Downers Grove, IL: IVP Academic, 2015), both of which provide theologically grounded, clinically informed, and academically rigorous discussion.

2. Kendra Cherry, "Freud's Psychosexual Stages of Development," VeryWellMind, updated July 24, 2019, http://www.verywellmind.com/freuds-stages-of-psychosexual-development-2795962.

3. Deb Hirsch, "The Church's Sex Problem," *OnFaith*, July 21, 2016, https://www.onfaith.co/onfaith/2015/08/06/the-churchs-sex-problem/37513.

4. Debra Hirsch, *Redeeming Sex: Naked Conversations About Sexuality and Spirituality* (Downer's Grove, IL: InterVarsity Press, 2015), 66–67.

5. Joy Beth Smith, *Party of One: Truth, Longing, and the Subtle Art of Singleness* (Nashville: Nelson Books, 2018), 82.

6. Hirsch, "Church's Sex Problem."

7. Hirsch notes that Origen later renounced his literal reading of "and there are also eunuchs who made themselves eunuchs for the sake of the kingdom" (Matt. 19:12), and she comments this was "a bit late perhaps for the offending organs!" *Redeeming Sex*, 34.

8. New Testament Greek has a perfectly good word for the body, which is *soma*. *Soma* refers to the physical, corporeal nature of a person. "Take, eat, this is my body [*soma*]," said Jesus. Paul actually uses both *soma* and *sarx*, which means we need to consider the meaning he intends for each, rather than assuming they're synonyms. In Greek, *sarx* can mean "meat," but the fact that Paul uses *sarx* repeatedly as a contrast to the kingdom "life of the Spirit" suggests he intends *sarx* to convey far more than just "meat." Meat is hardly the opposite of the abundant, eschatological life of the kingdom that Paul is describing. For additional background, see Tara M. Owens, *Embracing the Body: Finding God in Our Flesh and Bone* (Downer's Grove, IL: InterVarsity Press, 2015), 93–94.

9. Lauren Winner, "Lauren Winner on Real Sex," interview by Kristen McCarty, *RELEVANT*, July 12, 2005, https://relevantmagazine.com/life/relationship/features/3134-lauren-winner-on-real-sex.

10. Owens, *Embracing the Body*, 46.

11. Winner, "Lauren Winner on Real Sex."

12. Hirsch, *Redeeming Sex*, 42.

CHAPTER 3: BROTHERS, SISTERS, AND THE FAMILY OF GOD

1. I grew up thinking the word "helper," as it was used in Genesis, meant something like "assistant" or "executive secretary" at best. The helper was a "second," a backup or gopher, there to help the first with whatever was needed. I learned later that the Hebrew word for helper is *ezer*, and that it is used most often in the

Bible to describe God himself (Deut. 33:29; Ps. 33:20; 70:5; Hos 13:9). Learning that God was an *ezer* (a strong helper) to Israel dignified and recalibrated my understanding of the first human partnership. *Kenegdo* conveys the idea of being a "comparable" or "suitable" helper. Dogs might be man's best friend and horses can help pull a load, but only Eve was perfectly suited to the co-ruling, stewarding, and procreating tasks God gave to humanity. Men and women are both needed to fulfill God's mission in the world, and women are neither secondary nor sidekicks. For additional background, see Alice Mathews, *Gender Roles and the People of God* (Grand Rapids, MI: Zondervan, 2017), 39.

2. Mathews describes the first human pair as "God's A-team for his new world." *Gender Roles*, 36.

3. R. P. Kingdon, "Family," in *New Dictionary of Theology*, ed. Sinclair B. Ferguson, David F. Wright, and J. I. Packer (Downer's Grove, IL: Intervarsity Press, 1988), 250.

4. See Deut. 25:5–10, which also provides the theological backdrop for the book of Ruth. I really like my brother-in-law, but I think both he and I are grateful this law will never apply to us.

5. Catholic doctrine, which holds to Mary's perpetual virginity, has alternate explanations for Matt. 1:25, which speaks of how Joseph did not "know" (in the euphemistic sense of sex) Mary until after she brought forth her firstborn son. "Firstborn means having been born first and never implies the birth of others," explains the NKJV footnote. I find the textual evidence for Jesus having other natural-born siblings more persuasive, but even if one holds to the Catholic view, the fact remains that Jesus was part of a broader family whom he loved and to whom he was responsible. The Jewish understanding of "family" is broader than our modern conception of the mom-dad-two-kids-under-one-roof nuclear family.

6. David Seccombe, *The King of God's Kingdom: A Solution to the Puzzle of Jesus* (Milton Keynes: Paternoster, 2002), 351.

7. How YHWH became "Jehovah" is one of my favorite bits of nerdy Bible language history. The short version is this: written

Hebrew has only consonants. Hence God's name was written *YHWH*. But the name was considered too holy to say, so where *YHWH* was written, readers would substitute the name *Adonai* (meaning "lord"). At some point, the vowels of Adonai were superimposed onto *YHWH*, making the linguistically awkward *YaHoWaH*. And if you pronounce that with German consonants where *Y*s are *J*s and *W*s are pronounced as *V*s, you get *JaHoVaH*.

8. Philadelphia, often referred to as the "City of Brotherly Love," gets its name from a combination of two Greek words: *phileo* ("love and affection") + *adelphos* ("brother") = brotherly love.

9. Michael D. Marlowe, "The Translation of Αδελφος and Αδελφοι: A Response to Mark Strauss and I. Howard Marshall," Bible Research, 2004, http://www.bible-researcher.com/adelphos.html.

10. Rebecca Card-Hyatt, "Footnoted: Was the Bible Written Only for Men? Part 1," Junia Project, November 29, 2013, https://juniaproject.com/footnoted-bible-written-for-men-part-1/.

11. D. A. Carson, *The Inclusive Language Debate: A Plea for Realism* (Grand Rapids, MI: Baker, 1998), 130, 131.

12. Ed Stetzer, "Gender and the Christian Standard Bible: Trevin Wax Answers My Questions," *Christianity Today*, June 12, 2017, https://www.christianitytoday.com/edstetzer/2017/june/gender-hscb-csb-christian-standard-bible.html.

13. It's been over forty years since the *Star Wars* trilogy was released, and the statute of limitations on spoilers has surely passed. But still, forgive me for this reveal if you weren't expecting it. I won't say a word about who you-know-who's father is.

14. *Star Wars Episode IV: Return of the Jedi*, directed by Richard Marquand, written by George Lucas (San Rafael, CA: Lucasfilm, 1983).

15. N. T. Wright, *After You Believe: Why Christian Character Matters* (San Francisco: HarperOne, 2010), 184.

16. Wesley Hill, *Spiritual Friendship: Finding Love in the Church as a Celibate Gay Christian* (Grand Rapids, MI: Brazos Press, 2015), 58.

17. Hill, *Spiritual Friendship*, 60.

CHAPTER 4: WWJD, RELATIONAL SPHERES, AND VENN DIAGRAMS

1. Seccombe, *King of God's Kingdom*, 474.
2. Adam K. Levy (@adamklevy), Venn diagram image, Twitter, August 20, 2018, 1:34 p.m., http://twitter.com/adamklevy/status /1031640764747534336, used with permission.
3. Hill, *Spiritual Friendship*, 113.
4. Winner, *Real Sex*, 144.
5. Winner, 145, 146.

CHAPTER 5: IS MY SPOUSE MY SIBLING OR MY SOUL MATE?

1. As the members of the Roaring 20s fellowship bonded over the years, we began celebrating many thirtieth birthdays. At some point, a name change was suggested to better reflect our demographic. "What could possibly come after a name like the Roaring 20s?" Our brilliant friend Sarah observed, "Should we call it the Great Depression?" We left the name as it was.
2. I love what Lore Wilbert says about this: "We don't treat our marriage like it's the place where we can be our worst selves. We don't treat our home like it's the place where we can 'be real,' as though every other relationship in our lives deserves the fruit of the Spirit, but at home we can drop the facade and level all the pent-up frustration of the day at one another. [My husband] should get my best self, the best of the Spirit's fruit in my life and heart, not the worst self." Lore Wilbert, "Have This Mind Among You," Sayable, January 30, 2019, https://www.sayable.net/blog/2019/1/30/ have-this-mind-among-you.
3. For fellow fiction lovers, Alain du Botton's *The Course of Love* is a beautiful and painfully honest exploration of how romantic ideals betray and disappoint us in marriage.
4. Lauren Winner makes a surprising application on what lessons marriage can teach here: "Insofar as marriage is essentially an opportunity to learn, in concentrated form with one person,

what being a sibling in Christ means, married people can instruct single people in some slices of the sibling relationship." *Real Sex*, 146.

5. John Green, "Chubby Bunny . . . Blergh," 2:27, YouTube video published by vlogbrothers on February 14, 2011, https://www.youtube.com/watch?v=ma9AnIfaE30.

6. Knowing that a four-hundred-page treatise on the theology of marriage was probably not something I could recommend to many, I was thrilled when Christopher Ash published a shorter version. *Married for God: Making Your Marriage the Best It Can Be* (Wheaton, IL: Crossway, 2016) is a fantastic, and very readable, resource.

7. Stanford Gibson, "Failure Mode Analysis: Disaster Proofing Your Romantic Relationship," Preaching Transcripts and MP3s (blog), February 19, 2012, http://stanfordtranscripts.blogspot.com/2012/01/failure-mode-analysis-disaster-proofing.html.

CHAPTER 6: CAN MEN AND WOMEN BE JUST FRIENDS?

1. Tina Osterhouse, "Why Christians Can Do Better Than the 'Billy Graham Rule,'" CBE International, April 4, 2017, https://www.cbeinternational.org/blogs/why-christians-can-do-better-billy-graham-rule.

2. Wilkin, "3 Female Ghosts."

3. Wesley Hill, "Love, Again: On a Celibate Breakup and What Happened After," *Comment*, May 10, 2018, https://www.cardus.ca/comment/article/love-again/.

4. Tammy Perlmutter, "Same-Sex Attraction and Me," Mudroom, March 1, 2017, http://mudroomblog.com/same-sex-attraction-and-me/.

5. Ann Smith, "What I Learned from Same-Sex Abuse Inside the Church," *Christianity Today*, September 11, 2018, https://www.christianitytoday.com/women/2018/september/same-sex-church-abuse-what-i-learned-from-my-case.html.

6. Kate Shellnut, "I Didn't Marry My Best Friend," *Christianity*

Today, September 15, 2014, https://www.christianitytoday.com
/ct/2014/september/i-didnt-marry-my-best-friend.html.

7. Joy Beth Smith, "Flying Solo in a Family-Centered Church,"
book review of Gina Dalfonzo's *One by One*, *Christianity Today*,
May 25, 2017, https://www.christianitytoday.com/ct/2017/june
/flying-solo-in-family-centered-church.html.

8. This statement of Paul's in 1 Cor. 7:9 is often taken out of context.

9. C. S. Lewis described recognition when he wrote, "Friendship.
. . is born at the moment when one man says to another 'What!
You too? I thought that no one but myself. . . .'" *The Four Loves*
(New York: HarperCollins, 1960), 100.

10. John Townsend and Henry Cloud's works—including their
books *Boundaries*, *Safe People*, and *Changes That Heal*—are some
of the excellent resources available for helping us discern what
healthy relationships look like in expectations and conflict.
Townsend and Cloud's works are the gold standard when it
comes to literary litmus tests for love.

11. Wesley Hill, "Jigs for Marriage and Celibacy," *Comment*,
November 24, 2016, https://www.cardus.ca/comment/article
/jigs-for-marriage-and-celibacy/.

12. Ty Grigg, "How I Learned to Stop Worrying About the Billy
Graham Rule and Love Like Jesus," Missio Alliance, July 18,
2014, https://www.missioalliance.org/how-i-learned-to-stop
-worrying-about-the-billy-graham-rule-and-love-like-jesus/.

13. Grigg, "How I Learned to Stop Worrying."

CHAPTER 7: WHAT ABOUT ALL THE HORROR STORIES?

1. Hill, "Jigs for Marriage."

2. Philip Yancey, *What's So Amazing About Grace?* (Grand Rapids,
MI: Zondervan, 1997), 206.

3. Karen Swallow Prior, "The Problem with 'Don't Eat Alone with
Women': Good Character Is Better Than Strict Rules," Vox,
April 1, 2017, https://www.vox.com/first-person/2017/4/1
/15142744/mike-pence-billy-graham-rule.

4. See Prov. 3:13; 4:5, 7; 16:16; 19:20; Ecc. 7:25; James 1:5.

5. Alice Mathews, *Gender Roles and the People of God: Rethinking What We Were Taught About Men and Women in the Church* (Grand Rapids, MI: Zondervan, 2017), 75.

6. Ed Stetzer, "It's Abuse, Not an Affair, and It Appears We Need to Be Reminded . . . Again," *Christianity Today*, June 16, 2014, https://www.christianitytoday.com/edstetzer/2014/june/its -abuse-not-affair.html.

7. Monica Lewinsky, "'Who Gets to Live in Victimville?': Why I Participated in a New Docuseries on *The Clinton Affair*," *Vanity Fair*, November 13, 2018, https://www.vanityfair.com/news /2018/11/the-clinton-affair-documentary-monica-lewinsky.

8. Morgan Lee, "Max Lucado Reveals Past Sexual Abuse at Evangelical #MeToo Summit," *Christianity Today*, December 13, 2018, https://www.christianitytoday.com/news/2018/december /metoo-evangelicals-abuse-beth-moore-caine-lucado-gc2 -summit.html.

9. Andy Crouch, "It's Time to Reckon with Celebrity Power," Gospel Coalition, March 24, 2018, https://www .thegospelcoalition.org/article/time-reckon-celebrity-power/.

10. Justin Taylor, "Where Did the 'Billy Graham Rule' Come From?," Gospel Coalition, March 30, 2017, https://www .thegospelcoalition.org/blogs/evangelical-history/where-did -the-billy-graham-rule-come-from/.

11. Lauren Collins, "What Would Billy Do?," *New Yorker*, April 10, 2017, https://www.newyorker.com/magazine/2017/04/10/virtue -and-vice-mike-pences-dining-policy.

12. Nancy Beach, quoted by Lee, "Max Lucado."

13. Karen Swallow Prior, *On Reading Well: Finding the Good Life Through Great Books* (Grand Rapids, MI: Brazos Press, 2018), 34.

14. Crouch, "Celebrity Power."

CHAPTER 8: WILL YOU DRIVE WITH ME?

1. Perhaps one reason arranged marriages have fared as well as—or in many cases, better than—love matches is that those doing the arranging are pairing people who share many cultural and

familial similarities, which would make "road trip expectations" pretty compatible. Two children of country-music-loving families, both raised on yearly summer fishing trips at the lake, won't be shocked, then, if their road trip partner turns on their country music playlist and suggests a detour to a tackle shop. Just a theory. Of course, any couple can learn each other's preferences and idiosyncrasies, but there is some *ease* that comes from pairings in which there is already considerable cultural/experiential overlap.

2. Winner, *Real Sex*, 106.

3. As someone born and raised in the Southern Hemisphere, I've sometimes wondered why "going south" is a synonym for things going badly. Is this a vestige of colonialism showing its Northern Hemisphere privilege? But I digress.

4. Winner, *Real Sex*, 107.

5. Linda and Charlie Bloom, "Want More and Better Sex? Get Married and Stay Married," July 13, 2017, HuffPost, https:// www.huffpost.com/entry/want-more-and-better-sex-get -married-and-stay-married_b_5967b618e4b022bb9372aff2.

CHAPTER 9: WHERE DO WE GO FROM HERE?

1. *Merriam-Webster*, s.v. "stewardship," https://www.merriam -webster.com/dictionary/stewardship.

2. Marlena Graves, "Our Sexuality in Reality," Mudroom, March 22, 2017, http://mudroomblog.com/our-sexuality-in-reality/.

3. Winner, *Real Sex*, 134.

4. Cutter Kallaway, *Breaking the Marriage Idol* (Downer's Grove, IL: IVP Books, 2018), 147.

5. Graves, "Our Sexuality in Reality."

6. Winner, *Real Sex*, 30.

7. "II. The Vocation to Chastity," *Catechism of the Catholic Church*, 2nd ed. (New York: Doubleday, 1995), 620–21.

8. Graves, "Our Sexuality in Reality."

9. Hill, *Spiritual Friendship*, 81.

10. Callaway, *Breaking the Marriage Idol*, 17.

11. Winner, *Real Sex*, 141.
12. D. H. Field, "Sexuality," in *New Dictionary of Theology*, 638.
13. In a chilling article detailing how genocide has distinct social and psychological stages, Dr. Gregory Stanton, president of Genocide Watch, lists the first stage as "classification," in which language is used to separate one group from another. It's *us* versus *them*. The fourth stage is "dehumanization," which again deploys language to describe "those" groups as animals, vermin, criminals, or whatever other term is employed in propaganda. "The Ten Stages of Genocide," Genocide Watch, accessed August 10, 2019, http://www.genocidewatch.org/genocide/tenstagesofgenocide.html.
14. Claire Cameron, "5 Languages That Could Change the Way You See the World," *Nautilus*, March 3, 2015, http://nautil.us/blog/5-languages-that-could-change-the-way-you-see-the-world.
15. Krish Kandiah, "Church Is a Family, Not an Event," *Christianity Today*, December 28, 2018, https://www.christianitytoday.com/ct/2019/january-february/church-as-family-not-event-kandiah.html.
16. Field, "Sexuality," 639.
17. Kandiah, "Church Is a Family."
18. Kandiah, "Church Is a Family."
19. Kandiah, "Church Is a Family."

ABOUT THE AUTHOR

Bronwyn Lea has been active for twenty years in vocational ministry to serve, encourage, teach, and mobilize Christians of all ages. A graduate of law school and seminary, she ministers in her local church and also heads up *Propel Sophia*, the Christian-living wisdom resource for Propel Women. Bronwyn is mom to three school-aged kids, who keep her somewhere between hilarious laughter and desperate prayer on any given day. She and her fellow South African husband live in Northern California, where they count the men and women in their church as both friends and family. Find out more at www.bronlea.com.